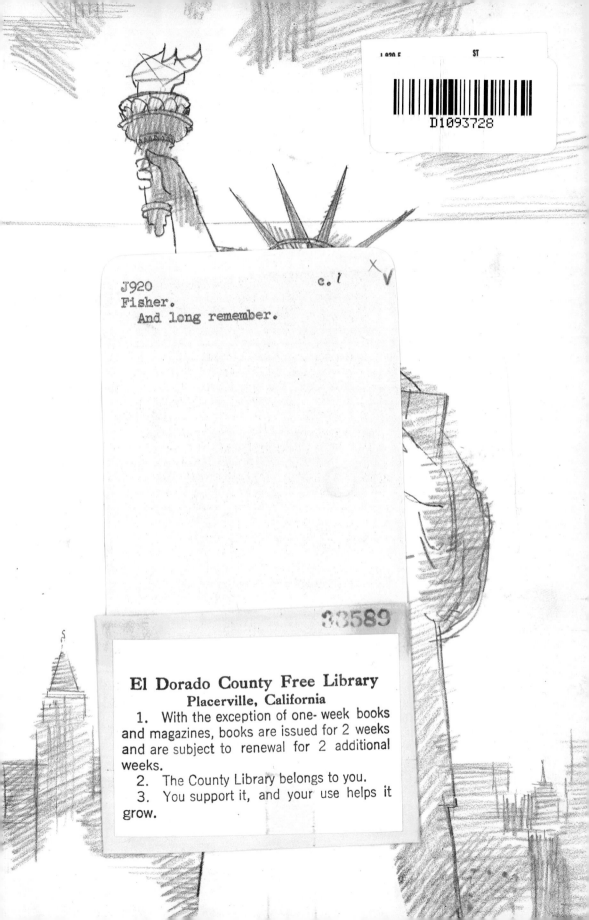

AND LONG REMEMBER

Some Great Americans Who Have Helped Me

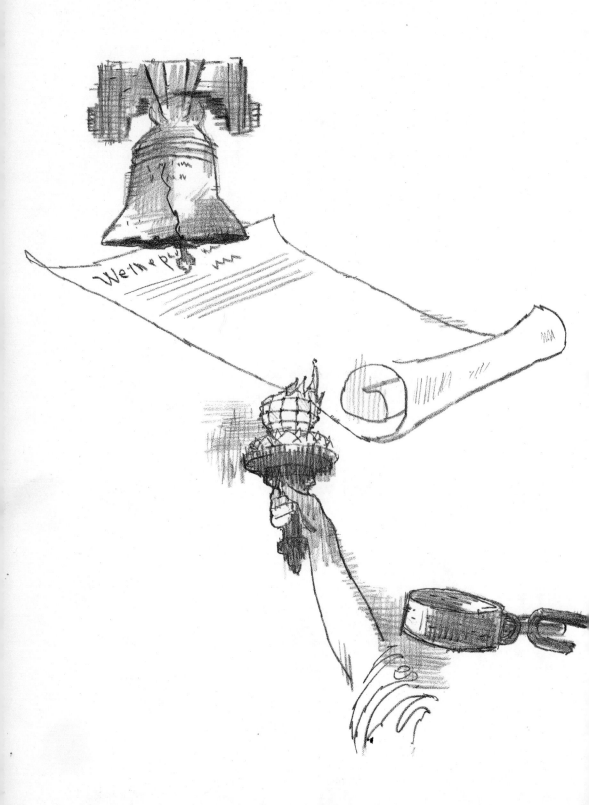

AND LONG REMEMBER

Some Great Americans Who Have Helped Me

DOROTHY CANFIELD FISHER

Illustrated by EZRA JACK KEATS

WHITTLESEY HOUSE
McGraw-Hill Book Company, Inc.
NEW YORK   TORONTO   LONDON

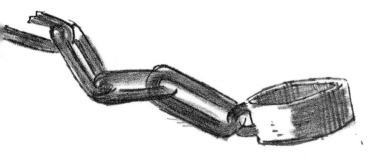

Library of Congress Catalog Card Number: 59–11929

Published by Whittlesey House
A division of the McGraw-Hill Book Company, Inc.

Preparation of this book was interrupted by the author's
final illness. Her list of American heroes and heroines was
a long one and she had planned to include others in this
volume (Thoreau, Emerson, President and Mrs. Franklin
D. Roosevelt and President Dwight D. Eisenhower, to
mention a few).

While Mrs. Fisher made every effort to avoid inaccuracy,
she did not feel bound to discard some memorable phrases
which, though they rest on scanty evidence, ring true to
the American spirit at its best and have therefore become
part of our national heritage.

CONTENTS

This book is affectionately dedicated to
Helene Frye

Also by Dorothy Canfield Fisher

A FAIR WORLD FOR ALL: The Meaning of the Declaration of Human
Rights

OUR INDEPENDENCE AND THE CONSTITUTION

PAUL REVERE AND THE MINUTE MEN

UNDERSTOOD BETSY

Adult Books and Anthologies

THE BENT TWIG

THE DEEPENING STREAM

FOUR-SQUARE

HARVEST OF STORIES

LEARN OR PERISH

MADE-TO-ORDER STORIES

MEMORIES OF ARLINGTON, VERMONT

AND LONG REMEMBER

Some Great Americans Who Have Helped Me

When I was a girl on vacation-visits to the family farm, my great-uncle spent a lot of patient effort teaching me how to harness and drive a team of work horses. As things turned out that particular bit of knowledge has never been of the least practical use to me. Is it fair then to say that he was just wasting his time and mine? No! That answer would miss one of the real benefits which learning—learning almost anything thoroughly—brings to us. All the drill in finding the right buckle for each strap, the mental habit built up through solving a problem piece by piece, step by step, must have made it easier for me later on when I had to change a flat tire on some lonely back road.

And knowing about old-time customs and wisdom can do a great deal more than just training our hands and brains to work at jobs in an orderly manner. Ever since the dawn of history, when our cavemen ancestors invented words to express their thoughts, old people have been trying to pass on whatever experience has taught them about ideas of right and wrong, about what sort of actions bring lasting satisfaction—in the hope of helping the boys and girls around them who are just starting out in life for themselves. Often enough what fathers and mothers have to say seems out of date. Their memories of the past do not fit today's changed conditions. And anyone can see that the future promises to be strange beyond the wildest flights of our present imagination.

But just the same it is foolish and self-defeating for us to shut our eyes to everything that happened before we were born. For some things do *not* change. Water will run downhill in the future as it always has. Fire will burn. And as we look back into the story of humanity we see that there have always been elements in our own human nature which have persisted in spite of all the prodigious differences in the outer circumstances of life from century to century.

Some of these elements are nothing to be proud of, because we human beings have a mixed inheritance. As we read the pages of history we can easily be discouraged by finding so many examples of greed and cruelty, the struggle for riches and power at no matter what cost of suffering to others. But this is only part of the picture.

For, when we say that the inherited urges in the human blood stream are mixed, we don't in the least mean to deny that some of those deep-rooted urges are better—enormously better—than others. Any child *may* grow up to be a gangster; the fact is that only two or three in every thousand do become criminals. The overwhelming majority of young people now in school are going to turn out pretty much like their fathers, mothers, great and great-great-grandparents—reasonably good average citizens. *But* (and it is a big "but") in the future as in the past, a few will rise far above the general average, a few will carry on the great tradition handed down to them by those earlier men and women whose main motive was not to seek advantage for themselves, who actually forgot themselves most of the time because their minds were entirely occupied with something bigger—perhaps organizing a working government to provide liberty and justice for all, perhaps finding a cure for diphtheria, protesting against slavery, or puzzling out as best they could the reasons for the tides, the trade winds, and eclipses of the sun and moon.

This tells us something about what we human beings really care for deep down in our hearts, that in the long run the vast majority of people all over the world have come to believe such unselfish actions are worthwhile, that they are expressions of intelligence and character at its highest level. And it proves to us that such ideals are not just impractical visions about what life might be, that they are not invented myths about heroes and saints of antiquity, when we find that throughout the short span of our national history there have been plenty of men who have actually put these ideals into practice, and by acting on them in one way or another have made their lives tremendously valuable to anybody and everybody.

Consider the example of Benjamin Franklin. By early middle age he had made enough from his writing and his printing shop to retire with a comfortable income. He was a good mixer. Everybody liked and admired him. Did he sit back and settle down to a life of ease? No, he did not. He took on and carried through, one after another, laborious tasks that helped the Colonies win their independence and establish a new nation.

George Washington Carver, the orphan Negro boy, with little help beyond his native intelligence, resolution, and hard work, made himself an outstanding authority on plant growth, plant diseases, plant uses as food and as raw material for a long string of industrial products. He was offered many well-paid teaching positions in the North. He refused them all politely and went instead to struggling Tuskegee Institute, so cramped for money that it could afford no laboratory equipment at all, but did offer him the chance to use his great talents in helping his long-oppressed, newly-emancipated race to take the first necessary steps toward healthy self-support.

After the Civil War the General-in-Chief of the Confederate Army had suffered a blow which might well have crushed a life-time officer, son of a proud Virginia family. The Old South was ruined. Very well then, a New South must be built up, and those who were to build it needed education. With neither bitterness nor bravado Robert E. Lee rode his horse over the mountains into the Shenandoah Valley and until his death carried on his new duties as president of the small college which was to become Washington and Lee University.

Now what do we mean when we say that these men and others like them gave something valuable to the world? Why are some things valuable and others not? That question used to puzzle me when I was young. This is how I found an answer to it:

Late one winter afternoon I happened to be walking through a poor section of a big city, when suddenly the people around me began to shout "Fire!" and wave their arms, pointing toward an old brick five-story tenement house. Sure enough. Frightened tenants were running out, with clouds of smoke following them through the open front door. The windowpanes, lit up by the flames behind them, glowed red and yellow. Then I heard sirens screaming, and down the avenue raced the fire trucks.

The police pushed the crowd back, but I was lucky enough to find a place on a nearby porch where I could see everything. Lines of hose were coupled to hydrants. Big streams of water began to shoot into all the lower floors. And now an enormously tall ladder was raised from one of the trucks, up and up, until it reached one of the highest windows. A fireman climbed it, so fast that he almost seemed to run. He smashed a window sash and went inside. We all held our breaths waiting until he came out and brought—what do you think he had saved? If it had been a bundle of somebody's stocks and bonds, or a diamond necklace, that would have been worthwhile, I suppose, but nothing for us to get excited about. What he did carry was a baby, and a great roaring cheer went up from the crowd. I, too, was yelling my throat out with the rest. Why did we care so much? Because a baby was alive, and life is precious.

Right then it struck me that a noble act or word also has life in it. We must not let it die.

At times, during the last forty-odd years of hot wars and cold wars interspersed with periods of truce which were not peace, I might have lost the courage needed to face the bad news of today and the worse news threatening tomorrow if I had not remembered the life-giving ideas spoken or acted out by the long line of great citizens who have proved that human existence is not fated to be only a mad scramble of grab and guzzle. So now I want to share these memories with young people today, and to make the last book I shall ever write a collection of true, *true* stories about real people who have given us all a reason to feel proud that we too are Americans.

My list is by no means complete. Many, many more names deserve to be included. I have been forced to limit myself to a few whose messages have especially reassured and heartened me, who by the course of their lives, or sometimes by a single act or speech in a moment of crisis, have given me strength and faith.

I hope that if, with the world problems of the years to come, you sometimes feel as though you were being tossed about on a night flight in an airplane with storm clouds blotting out the stars, the memory of these great words and deeds will blaze out like a line of beacons showing you the right course through the darkness ahead.

Knowing the best of the past, you can face the future resolute and unafraid.

THE MAN WHO
HEARD LINCOLN

"The world will little note, nor long remember . . ."

Back in the eighteen eighties and nineties, when I was in the grades and high school, a great many of the elderly gray-haired men in any town where I lived or visited were ex-soldiers who had served in the Union Army. There were so many of them that hardly any of us noticed the Grand Army of the Republic button on the coat lapel of the postmaster, or the storekeeper, or the bank cashier. Naturally enough! For to my generation Bull Run was twice as many years back in the past as the Battle of the Bulge is to you.

But in our tiny village one veteran kept us from entirely forgetting the war and what it meant. Frank Hutton was a plain, ordinary sort of man who worked with his hands to earn a living. His neighbors respected him because he could be counted on to give back a fair return for his wages at building fence or digging ditches, because he was honest and paid his bills. Beyond that, most of the time no one gave him a thought. He had grown up in the days when education in American rural schools meant little more than learning by heart and reciting back to the teacher word by word what the textbook said about the fundamentals of readin', writin', and 'rithmetic. Only the brightest pupils (and Frank wasn't one of those) managed to keep all that rigmarole in their minds a minute after they had been given a passing grade. He wasn't a leader. When I knew him I doubt if he ever read anything to speak of . . . except maybe notices of old folks' funerals, new babies born, barns struck by lightning, in the local weekly newspaper. He was too shy to draw attention to himself even by calling out at Town Meeting, "I second the motion." No, there wasn't anything in the way he lived or talked that made him seem different from anybody else. He hadn't been wounded or fought in any of the big battles, as far as we knew. But once in a while we woke up to the fact that, after all, something about him was special. He was the only man we had ever met who had actually been there at the Gettysburg Dedication, and with his own ears heard Abraham Lincoln deliver one of the greatest speeches of all time.

For although Antietam and Shiloh were just names in the history book to us, the Gettysburg Address was real. It was alive. We all knew it, and some of us had the chance to stand up on the platform and recite it at Memorial Day celebrations. How our nerves used to tingle then! Like the Declaration of Independence with its "We hold these truths to be self-evident," or the Constitution's "We, the *people* of the United States," Lincoln's few short sentences seemed to lay the foundation stone for all our American hopes, aspirations, and ideals.

But what we thought of Frank Hutton was nothing compared to the way visitors from the outside carried on. I remember vividly the first time a professor from one of the big universities heard about Frank. He jumped up from the porch chair where he had been chatting with my father, slapped his breast pocket to make sure he had his notebook, and rushed off, calling back over his shoulder, "Why this is the opportunity of a lifetime. Flesh-and-blood, word-of-mouth history! What a chapter it will make in my new book!"

A long time later he came back and dropped silently into his chair at our supper table. Finally, when the evening train was just about due, he said good-bye and started to the station. My father walked with him and I trotted along behind. That was ages and ages ago, but the sound of his disheartened voice still rings in my ears as he answered my father's question: "No use. He didn't remember anything to the purpose. *Not a thing*. Impossible! Incredible!"

That was the start of a long procession, all ending the same way. As the word got around, from time to time some history teacher or writer would come to our home and ask directions for finding "the little house by the brook where the man lives. . . ."

We didn't wait for them to finish the question. We knew what they wanted. We took them to the corner of Stony Lane and pointed out the house. We also knew that they were going to waste their time, but we let them find that out for themselves.

They all did find that out, although some of them struggled hard before they would admit it. Old Frank was never impatient with them. He did his very best to dig up something that might help them. Yes, he was a green recruit at the time, had felt quite set up when the drill sergeant decided he knew the manual of arms and the rest of it well enough to be one of the honor guard. Yes, he remembered how they marched in and took their places around the speaker's platform. As they spaced themselves out in open order he found himself standing just in front of where the President was sitting . . . *exactly* in front it must have been because he heard the chair leg scrape when Mr. Lincoln got up and came forward to speak.

But old Frank continued as straightforward as he always had been. No amount of prompting by leading questions could coax or badger him into pretending that he remembered more than he really did.

"No, I didn't see how he looked . . . couldn't turn round, of course. I was on duty . . . never budged from 'Eyes front.'"

"How did his talk strike me? I couldn't just tell you about that. Seems like there were some figures at the start, and I never was good at figures. I sort of lost my bearings."

"Did the audience clap or gasp or stir around when they heard: 'It is for us the living, rather, to be here dedicated . . .'? Well now I can't rightly recollect them words. You see it was all over so quick. 'Tother fellow, he talked on and on, but Mr. Lincoln, he'd hardly got goin' before he sat down again. And all the while I was holding myself up stiff and straight so as to be a credit to the regiment like the sergeant said I should. And first thing I knew I heard the order to close ranks, and there we were in column again, a-marching off. I'd be glad to accommodate you if I could . . . only that's the every last bit that sticks in my mind."

As usual old Frank told the truth and nothing but the truth—as he saw it. That was the every last bit he had got out of his day at the Gettysburg cemetery.

Now, you may well be wondering why I am taking so much space to tell this story about a very uninteresting old man. Frank Hutton was all right so far as his ability went—only it didn't go very far. No doubt he would have given up his own life that day to prevent an assassin from killing President Lincoln. But that didn't happen. Quick, simple, heroic actions like that are called for very seldom in anyone's life. The chances are against our ever being put to such a test. The opportunity Frank Hutton missed was that he didn't even try to hear and understand the glorious message which was going past his ears. With his limited brains and training poor Frank couldn't understand.

But you can!

At least I hope you can. And in that hope I intend, chapter by chapter, to sketch out for you a few examples of great Americans who have set a high standard of citizenship for us to follow.

The book won't be worth reading if you get out of it nothing more than scraps of information, crammed into your minds haphazardly, like the disorderly, disconnected pages in a poorly kept loose-leaf notebook. I don't deny that facts are the basis of all knowledge. But facts—just by themselves, a few paragraphs copied out of an encyclopedia, some marks on a map locating Jamestown or Plymouth—won't take you more than the first short steps along the road to knowledge.

It is what facts mean that makes them important. That's what you must try to find out. The next time you reread the Gettysburg Address, try to think, and even more try to feel yourself back in the setting of that November day in 1863. Many of the spectators had lost a son or a husband on that very spot. The war had dragged along for twenty-seven terrible months of slaughter. No one could guess when or how it would end. Added to its burden, the constant demands of politicians asking fat jobs for their friends, the bickering between members of his Cabinet, the jealousy among high-ranking army officers weighed heavily on the

President's shoulders. Far from certain that the enemy would be beaten, he was not even sure of support from the war-weary Northern states. Only a few months before, a mob rioting against conscription had paralyzed law and order, burning and pillaging through the great city of New York for three whole days. In many other sections there was grumbling discontent, which would come to a heat at the next political campaign when the opposition party's platform was to begin with the open declaration that the war had been a failure. All this Abraham Lincoln knew as he sat on the platform waiting for his turn. And yet he found the strength to step forward and speak out the faith that was in him.

Against that background, can anyone read the words "we here highly resolve that these dead shall not have died in vain" without feeling an inner strength rise in him, without pledging to stand up bravely to whatever life may bring?

The big question is whether you can think and feel deeply enough about your nation's future. Everything depends on that, because together with other young people all over the United States you are going to make the future for better or for worse—because you are America's future.

Some older people tell me it is no use talking seriously to you. "No," they say, "these kids are only interested in basketball scores, and dates, and the latest thing in hair-dos."

I just don't believe them. It will take some thinking—maybe a lot, and some feeling—maybe a lot, before you can look right down to the real full inner spirit of some of the life histories printed here. But I am positive that you have what it takes to think—to feel—to understand—and so, when the time comes, to act.

But I can't prove that I am right without your help. Come along then! Let's go! *Together!*

GEORGE WASHINGTON

"... as a citizen of the great republic of humanity at large ..."

How old were you when you first began to know who George Washington was? Do you suppose you can remember as far back as that? Most Americans can't. It seems as if we'd always known about him—the Father of Our Country.

It would be foolish for me to repeat once more what you and everyone else ought to have read many times—that he commanded the American Revolutionary Army, was first President of the United States, and all the rest of it. So here, and everywhere in this book when I am writing about a famous person, I intend to leave out most of the information easily found in the library and tell you only some particular incidents or traits of character which might not be found easily but which—for me at least—give that person a special and unusual claim to our love and admiration.

So now let's pass over Valley Forge and Yorktown, and start with a question: Did you ever think that George Washington never had any children? He never said anything about this—he never did say much about his feelings. What he felt was shown by what he did. For, somehow, his big house always had children in it. He married a widow, mother of a little boy and girl. Kindly and gentle, Washington helped care for them. And at different times he took into his home nine other children who were related to him in some way.

But the son whom Washington would have been so glad to have as his own came to him from across the ocean, from France. His name was Lafayette.

Lafayette was born in a rich family in France, and was a lord with a title—Marquis. Nobody around him expected him to do any work, but to live on the money he inherited, to go hunting, play cards, and spend a lot of time going to parties at court.

What he did do, as a boy of nineteen, was to run away and set sail for the wild, unknown continent of North America, to help the people there fighting for the right to make their own laws and run their own country.

When he left France on that sailing ship, he didn't know any English at all, but he learned all he could on his journey. It took weeks and weeks to cross the Atlantic in a sailing ship, so when he landed at a southern port he spoke English well enough to get along. He bought a horse, rode nine hundred miles north to Philadelphia, and told the American Congress there that he had come to fight with them for independence.

George Washington liked the young man at sight, and took him home with him. From that time on, the two were close to each other. To Lafayette more than to anybody else, Washington said what he really felt and hoped.

The war between the American Colonies and the British went on, with all the ups and downs which we study in our history books. Lafayette was mostly with Washington at his headquarters. But sometimes he fought as an officer in the battles. He was wounded in the Battle of Brandywine.

The silent George Washington spoke out then as he seldom did. To the army surgeon he said, "Take care of him as if he were my own son. For I love him as such." As Lafayette got better, George Washington often went for long talks in his sickroom.

Finally, eight years after Lafayette had come to give his services, and his life if need be, to the cause of liberty, the Colonies had won the war. The United States was founded.

To us, that's one of the greatest events in history. Closely following it in France, there occurred another one of the greatest events in history—the French Revolution. By that time, Lafayette was back in France, once more on the side of human freedom.

George Washington was very tired after the terrific years of trying to win a war with too little money and too few troops, and Lafayette was in the midst of a violent revolution. You might have thought they would have lost touch with each other. But no. They never stopped loving each other like father and son, and letters often passed between them.

In these letters we often can see what Washington, deep down in his heart, was feeling. For instance, in a letter of 1783 Washington spoke about a plan of Lafayette's for helping Negroes move forward into a free future. "I am all in favor of your scheme to encourage emancipation of the black people—I shall be happy to join you in so laudable a work." When, years later, Washington's will was read after his death, it was almost as if he were still writing to his adopted son, for the first clause, the very first, was to free his slaves.

But perhaps one of the most important things that Washington wrote to Lafayette was about international trade.

You see, as long as the Americans were colonists, England made the laws; and these laws forbade Americans to manufacture much of anything, even for their own use. They also made it hard for Americans to sell their raw materials to any nation except England. Timber, grain, hides, pig iron, pitch, turpentine, for instance, were sold at the low prices always paid for such raw materials. Then the Americans were supposed to buy from England the products—steel, glass, pottery, hats, fine woolen cloth—made by skilled English workers. Such manufactured products always sell for more than raw materials. It was an excellent business arrangement—for the English.

Now that America was independent and could do anything she wanted to, Washington was convinced that it would be better all around if trade were free in an open market. The more countries traded goods with each other, the better. That was what *he* thought and wrote to Lafayette.

"There are many articles of manufacture which we stand absolutely in need of. And we shall have large quantities of timber, fish, oil, tobacco, indigo, etc., to dispose of. We find the quality and prices of the French goods we receive to be better in many instances than the quality and price of the English. However unimportant America may be considered at present, there will assuredly come a day when this country will have some weight in the scale of empires. Your successful endeavor, to promote the interests of your two countries (as you justly call them) must give you the most unadulterated satisfaction; be assured that the measures which have lately been taken in France with regard to the two articles of oil and tobacco have intended very much to endear you to your fellow-citizens on this side of the Atlantic."

So far this had been, you see, just a straight business letter, stressing the material value of free, open commercial connections between France and the U.S. But here Washington, as if he felt that he and his adopted French son were once again talking freely with one another, began to write of a deeper meaning which, he

24

hoped, international commerce might have, in the long run. "Although I pretend to no particular information respecting commercial affairs nor any foresight into the scenes of futurity," he wrote in the stately book-words of his period, "yet (if I may be allowed the expression) *as a citizen of the great republic of humanity at large,* I cannot avoid reflecting with pleasure on the probable influence that commerce may often have on human manners and society in general. On these occasions I consider how mankind may be connected like one great family in fraternal ties. I indulge a fond idea that the period is not very remote when the benefits of a liberal and full commerce will pretty generally succeed to the devastations and horrors of war."

George Washington thus opened his heart and mind to the idealistic young Frenchman in 1786. A long time ago! We can thank Lafayette that we can hear Washington's very voice in our ears saying that he finds grounds for hope that in peaceful trading with each other, the nations of the future may forget war.

To that same open-hearted freedom with which he spoke to Lafayette we owe that noble phrase of his that he felt himself "a citizen of the great republic of humanity at large."

Don't you think—I do—that on the whole we modern Americans have a right to feel that Washington would approve of our effort to trade with all the nations of the world, and of our backing up the United Nations? The next time you see that familiar, dignified, serious face hanging in a frame on the wall, just stop and look up at it for a minute. I think you'll feel you have the right to say to him, "Well, Washington, we're doing our best to live up to you."

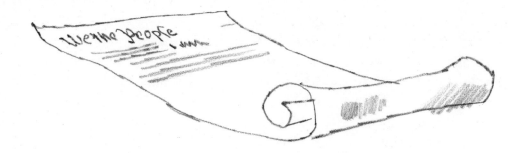

THOMAS JEFFERSON

". . . eternal hostility against every form of tyranny over the mind of man."

Thomas Jefferson served eight years in the Virginia Legislature before and during the Revolutionary War. In 1776 the Continental Congress adopted his famous Declaration of Independence. He was twice Governor of his state, went back for another term in Congress, spent five years in France as our ambassador, came home to be George Washington's Secretary of State. He was Vice-president in John Adams' administration, and when he was elected for two full terms as President, from 1800 to 1808, he doubled the size of the United States by buying the Louisiana territory from France. He also laid our claim to ownership of what afterwards became the states of Idaho, Oregon, and Washington by sending Lewis and Clark on an exploring expedition across the Rockies to the Pacific Ocean. Finally, after over forty years of almost continuous public service, he retired to his home, Monticello, where the land begins to slope up toward the Blue Ridge Mountains. There he did most of the work in organizing the still-flourishing University of Virginia.

And that is only part, and the least important part, of his life-work. President Wilson was right when he wrote, "The immortality of Thomas Jefferson does not lie in any one of his achievements, but in his attitude toward life."

What was so very special about his attitude toward life? He answered that question early in the Declaration: "We hold . . . that all men are created equal." This statement did not mean that he thought everyone has the same amount of strength and brains. He knew better than that. He did believe that anyone can grow a little, and some can grow a great deal, in ability. And he wanted the government to promise to keep its hands off, to give everyone an equal chance to make the most out of life—*everyone*—even those whose grandfathers had not been governors of a colony or who didn't inherit big fortunes.

Nobody questions that idea today. It seems to us absolutely the right way to run our country. But in the last quarter of the eighteenth century it was startlingly new. Many of Jefferson's companions in the Continental Congress did not believe it. Oh, they voted for the Declaration, all right, because they were tired of being ruled by the English. But after the war, when it came to drawing up a plan of government for the new country, a great many of them were afraid to trust the people, the plain, ordinary working people, with much power. Even John Adams, that stout old patriot, thought that with a little tinkering the British Constitution, top-heavy with class privileges as it was, would fit American conditions very well. Alexander Hamilton, soon to be Washington's brilliant Secretary of the Treasury, openly proposed that the President, once elected, should stay in office as long as he lived, like a European king, that he should *appoint* the governors of states, and that his veto of any law should be final. Hamilton also wanted a Senate serving for life, made up of men who owned a good deal of property.

That was not the way Thomas Jefferson saw it. He never backed down an inch on the program he had laid out in the Declaration. He worked for a republic shared in and supported by all citizens—in which the government's only right to rule rested on "the consent of the governed."

Jefferson was convinced that his ideal republic would flourish best in a community of small, family-owned, family-operated farms. It would not work at all where big plots of many thousand acres

each belonged to a single owner. Naturally then, the condition of his native state worried him. For Virginia had kept close to the social patterns of Old England. It had not even followed the moderate changes taking place in the mother country. It had almost no manufacturers, and little commerce except selling the tobacco crop abroad. There wasn't much chance to earn a living unless you owned some land. And starting a new farm was getting harder and harder, thanks to a couple of ancient laws called "entail" and "primogeniture," which made it always difficult and sometimes impossible for the owner to sell any part of a fertile plantation, even if he wanted to. And it had always been taken for granted that when the father died, every bit of his real estate ought to pass on to his oldest son. Jefferson started right away to get these laws repealed.

Jefferson had no personal grudge against the system. It had treated him well. He had inherited big plantations from his father, and through his mother he had blood connections with many of the most exclusive "gentry" families. But he didn't hesitate to hurt his friends' feelings. Too much good land in too few hands meant no room for the plain dirt farmer—meant that all political power was held by a tight little circle of the very rich. So he went to work and it was not many years before he and his followers managed not only to wipe out the old laws but to get the principle established that in most cases all a dead man's property should be divided equally among his children. Even the daughters were to get a fair share.

When I say "Jefferson and his followers" I do not mean that he deserves only a small part of the credit. On the contrary, he deserves most of it. No reformer can accomplish anything unless he can persuade other people that his strange new ideas are right. These followers very often do a large part of the detail work in rounding up the votes needed to win success for the projects. But they never would start the campaign if they were not first inspired by the vision of a great leader. Thomas Jefferson was that sort of leader. He seldom made public speeches, and even when he was a candidate for high office he did not run around asking people to vote for him. He merely talked things over with his friends or wrote letters to them explaining what his plans were, if he were elected. The friends did the electioneering for him. That method would have been political suicide for a lesser man—it worked perfectly for Jefferson.

Another sore spot in Virginia customs was the established church. A great many of the newer settlers belonged to some other denomination. They were Baptists or perhaps Presbyterians or Quakers. But just the same they were all taxed to pay the salaries of Anglican ministers. If the laws had been enforced, anyone who did not go to the services of the State Church could have been fined. All this made Jefferson's blood boil. He believed with all his heart and soul what no American questions nowadays—that the government must not interfere with the freedom of anyone to follow the guidance of his own personal conscience. Once more it took several years to bring about the reform. But at last the "Statute of Virginia for Religious Freedom" was passed.

Jefferson was so proud of this achievement that he chose it as one of the three to be noted on his tombstone. The other two were the authorship of the Declaration of Independence and the founding of the University of Virginia. To be sure, Jefferson was not the first American to believe in religious freedom. Roger Williams, for example, had preached it a century earlier. But it was Jefferson who brought the question out into the open where everyone would have to make up his mind about it. For Virginia, the oldest colony and the largest state, had enormous influence in our early history. It was not by accident that four of our first five presidents were Virginia men.

He did not succeed so well with another of his ideas. In fact, he got nowhere with it. He was sure that the sort of government he wanted could not work well unless the people understood the questions they were voting on. "If a nation expects to be ignorant and free," he said, "it expects that which never was and never will be." So he proposed a complete chain of state-supported primary and high schools, with college scholarships provided for the boys with good minds and little money. There was even to be a free state library. It was far in advance of any educational system existing at that time—unfortunately, too far in advance. His measure never got through the legislature. But at least he did his best. He was on the right track, looking far into the future.

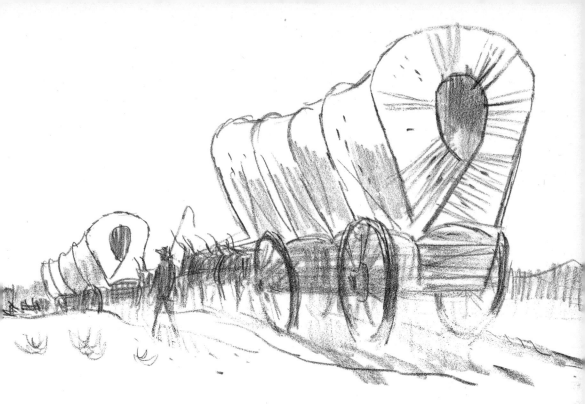

After the Revolution, settlers from the old seaboard states began to cross the Allegheny Mountains to find new homes in the broad lands stretching westward to the Mississippi River. Old claims to parts of this territory, based on the vague boundaries set down in Colonial charters, such as ". . . extending westward unto the South Sea," had been given up. And this act of farsighted, generous statesmanship left no question as to the ownership of the land. It was owned by the Congress of all the States acting together in the "Confederation" (our present Constitution had not yet been adopted).

So far everything was clear, but what next? How were those settlers to be governed? Were they for all time to be second-class citizens—colonists under the direction of some official in faraway Washington? It was Jefferson who drew up the first definite plan for their future. The whole territory was to be divided into sixteen sections. As soon as there were twenty thousand homemakers living in any of those sections they could organize a state government. And—no less important to Jefferson than the principle of self-government—there should be no slavery in any of the new states.

31

Congress could not make up its mind. First it passed this bill, then repealed it. But finally, three years later, it passed another ordinance changing the numbers required and forbidding slavery only in the country north of the Ohio River. But it kept the main idea—a government belonging to all citizens. A backwoodsman from Kentucky could take his seat in the national Senate beside a gentleman rice-planter from South Carolina. Either of them might cast the deciding ballot on some vital question of public policy. Thus as time went on state after state came into being, clear to the Pacific, each with all the rights of the first thirteen.

Why was Jefferson anxious to keep slavery out of the new states? He owned slaves on his plantation, didn't he? He was kind to them and they loved him. Nevertheless, like many others of the early Southern leaders, he was uneasy about the future. We know from his letters that he wished slaves had never been brought to America and would have welcomed any reasonable way to get rid of them. Was there such a way? He could see none. How could food be raised without them? In the Old South there was no free labor to take their places. His only hope was that slavery could be kept from spreading any further. Thousands of husbands and wives—the small landholders whom he described as "the most precious portion of the State"—must have room to build their log cabins and raise their children until they filled this rich new land in the Western territories. They must not be pushed back to scratch out a meager living on stony hillsides. Even though he got only half of what he asked for, his effort was not in vain. Seventy-seven years later what would have been the outcome if the men of Ohio, Indiana, Illinois, Michigan, Wisconsin, drawn by long familiarity with the plantation way of life, had supported the Confederacy? Instead they rallied to the cry, "Free soil! Free men!" and fought stoutly for the Union.

Slavery and the power it gave to owners of large plantations was not the only unhealthy element which Jefferson saw as a threat to his dream of a chance for all without help or hindrance from law or government. He felt bound to oppose concentration of political influence wherever it existed—in the rapidly growing shipping business, in banking. The longer the Federalist party stayed in office, the stronger grew its friendship for large financial interests. It seemed to have forgotten that the Constitution claimed to express the will of "We the people of the United States." Jefferson took those words at their face value. There must be a change, he thought. The administration at Washington should represent all the people, ditch diggers as well as bank presidents.

As the eighteenth century drew to a close, his keen insight about the movement of public opinion told him the time was ripe for a showdown. The campaign was fought out on fundamental issues. Half laughingly he described it to a friend: *they* (his opponents) were afraid of the ignorance of the people; *we* (his supporters) were even more afraid of the selfishness of the rulers, unless the people had a chance to hold them down.

The voters agreed with him. The result was a landslide. The party of restraint and reaction was crushed. In his inaugural address he put the same idea into a more polished form: "Some have said that Man cannot govern himself—can he then be trusted to govern others?" In plain words I suppose he meant that the people can—often do—make mistakes. But that no mistake is more tragic than the effort to force them into obeying an authority they do not respect.

His first term began tranquilly enough. Then he was called on to make a great decision. Often in wartime it happens that a general who has been advancing cautiously, according to a plan worked out by his staff, suddenly sees an opening where a total change in direction might smash through to victory. Shall he strike, or hold back and miss the golden chance? Jefferson faced such a problem in 1803. This was the situation:

More and more settlers were crossing the mountains, clearing the forests, raising big crops in the virgin soil. Kentucky was already a state, Ohio almost ready to be one. These pioneers needed many things—powder and shot for their hunting rifles, nails, pots and pans—and a long list of other items which they could not make for themselves. It was as true then as it is now that you couldn't buy unless you had money. These people had plenty to sell if they could get it to market. The steep rough trails leading back east were impossible for heavy loads. The one sure outlet was to the south by water. A brisk trade had started. Rafts and flatboats carried lumber and wheat down the many small rivers into the great Mississippi, and so to New Orleans. The west bank of the big river was owned by Spain, and at its mouth the Spaniards owned the land on both banks. However, a treaty allowed our boats free passage. Then, like a thunderbolt, came the news that the easy-going Spaniards had been forced to turn over both the western bank and the mouth of the Mississippi to France. And Napoleon, the French ruler, was a respecter of treaties only as long as it suited his own interests.

What was Jefferson to do? Nowhere could he find a clause directly authorizing either the President or Congress to spend a dollar out of the public treasury for a land purchase. He had always insisted that the power of the central government was limited to what was specifically granted it by the Constitution. He had always objected when others tried to stretch its powers beyond what was plainly allowed by the written words. But without help from Washington, these rugged, independent, frontier families needed to build up the American citizenship would be left at the mercy of a tyrant's whim. If river traffic stopped, what would happen? Their progress would be ended. They would drop back on a bleak struggle for day-by-day existence.

Jefferson now earned his title as a great commander. No matter which way he decided he would lose something he valued. Very well then, he would choose the way which offered the greatest gain for his country. He did not fold his hands and wait a year or more for the Constitutional amendment. He acted. He put aside his theory of legal limits to his power and did what had to be done. He sent a commission to Paris with authority to buy an island or a plot of ground on the lower Mississippi—whatever the French would sell, so long as it would give us a clear title to a harbor where the rivermen, protected by their own flag, could transfer their cargoes to ocean-going ships.

Months went by with no news. At last the commissioners came

back and reported.   For a while, they said, Napoleon had shown no interest.   Later, when he felt himself getting involved in a new European war, he had put the bargain on a take-it-or-leave-it, all-or-nothing basis.   They had greatly exceeded their instructions. They had bought everything France claimed to own in North America!   Still, under the circumstances, they hoped Mr. President would not disavow their act.

Mr. President took over full responsibility.   Congress went along with him, and appropriated the money.   All the plain people threw up their hats and shouted, "Hurrah!"

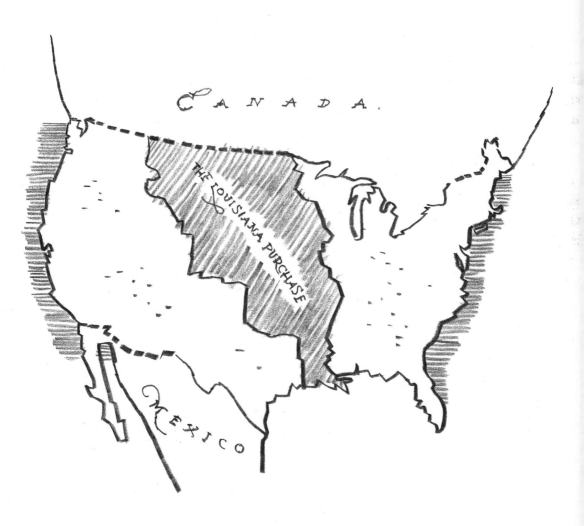

The price was fifteen million dollars, a big amount in those days. But let's look at a map of the United States and see what it bought. Put one tip of a ruler at the northern end of the boundary between Montana and Idaho. Then slant the ruler until it hits the Gulf of Mexico about one hundred miles west of New Orleans. That will give a rough idea of the territory involved . . . everything between the ruler and the Mississippi River—more open country than millions of homemakers could fill up.

There was hardly a branch of knowledge which Jefferson did not explore. He was rated the best architect of his time. He knew Latin, Greek, and French thoroughly, and had taught himself to read Spanish, Hebrew, Anglo-Saxon. He loved music, played the violin, and was an excellent horseman. He collected one of the very best early American libraries. He did not leave the volumes standing on their shelves. He read them—though I can't imagine how he found time for it.

He wrote a book about Virginia's native plants and animals, was interested in all sorts of scientific discoveries and theories. He experimented with rotation of crops on his plantations. I won't go on. To list and explain all the varied angles of his fine, rich, and far-reaching intelligence would fill a book. All I want to do here—if I can—is to try to show why his name stands very high in the list of those who have made the spirit of America what it is.

In its early uncertain days he steered our nation on its true course—toward liberty of thought, of speech, of religion. To his teaching we owe our faith that nothing more than a surface obedience to law and order can be enforced by the spies of a totalitarian police state—that rebellion is always smouldering in the hearts of slaves. For us, as for him, the only law and order worth having grows out of the self-discipline of free citizens.

Did any other of our Presidents match him? Yes, one—Abraham Lincoln. To show its gratitude toward these great leaders, our country has set up two memorial buildings in its capital city.

I remember so well that last time I was in Washington a group of boys and girls stopped their chatter and fun-making to stand in bright-eyed quiet as we all looked up into Lincoln's strong, sad face. I was sure that at least some of them were silently repeating —as I was—"This Government of the people, by the people, and for the people, shall not perish from the earth."

Then the group moved on and I followed, glad that these young strangers had been stirred by the nobility of that call to patriotism. Yet at the same time I was a little troubled as we walked along the springtime parkway. "It isn't fair to them," I was saying to myself. "There's more to it than that. Big questions where all the right seems on one side and the wrong on the other come up only once or twice in a lifetime. Wars and other calamities in public life— dictators like Mussolini and Hitler—can be prevented only if all our citizens do their level best to solve the little problems of every day. And that takes hard, honest thinking. It takes free discussion also, so that everyone can learn both sides and choose the better rather than the worse cause. Lincoln understood that. His life proves it. Jefferson protested against censorship in memorable words: "Error of opinion may be tolerated where reason is left free to combat it." "Oh, how I wish," I was thinking, "that young people could be reminded that only by the use of intelligence— only by constantly thinking and then thinking some more—have human beings risen step by step from barbarism."

Now we were going up the steps of the second memorial building, and there before us in great letters on the white marble I read the message I was looking for, as Thomas Jefferson wrote it a century and a half ago:

I HAVE SWORN ON THE ALTAR OF GOD ETERNAL HOSTILITY AGAINST EVERY FORM OF TYRANNY OVER THE MIND OF MAN.

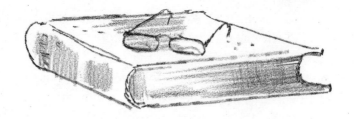

OLD DR. FRANKLIN

"He led a useful life."

We know so much about Benjamin Franklin's ingenious, generous and vital mind that it almost seems as if he were still alive, instead of dead for a hundred and seventy years. You probably were told some things about him long ago. And now very likely you are nodding your heads and thinking, "Oh, yeah—we learned all about old B.F. in the fifth grade."

Now let's stop a minute and consider what those words "all about him" amount to. Too often they add up to little more than these four items:

1. Poor Richard's prosy sayings, such as: "A penny saved is a penny earned," "Early to bed and early to rise, makes a man healthy and wealthy and wise," and a lot more of the same.

2. He was the stout old fellow with a bald head whose picture used to hang on the Assembly Room wall.

3. He signed the Declaration of Independence.

4. He flew a kite with a key fastened to its string and found out about lightning.

If your fifth-grade teacher made a specially good job of that lesson, maybe you also know that he was the first general postmaster in the thirteen English Colonies which later became the United States, and that he invented bifocal spectacles.

While this is all true, it is a pretty skimpy account of the man who thought up so many brilliant new ideas and served his country in so many different ways.

No, I am wrong. That list is not entirely true either. Because item one gives the impression that Poor Richard's sayings represent Franklin's own ideas about the best way to live. They do not. Poor Richard was just a made-up character, like one of those you might see in today's comic strips. Franklin invented him to add a touch of humor to the matter-of-fact information about weather, the position of the stars, the tides, the planting time for various crops, etc., in the yearly almanac he printed. The money-pinching advice of this old skinflint was never followed by his author after the first years when he was starting out in business without a dollar to his name. As soon as he began to be prosperous he contributed freely to all the churches in town, and to a great many other worthy organizations.

Though he was a keen businessman, he never drove a hard bargain. As a printer he did good work. Anything he wrote was read eagerly. Other authors at that time used complex sentences full of ponderous words with many syllables. Franklin had the gift for going straight to the point in clear plain English. One way or another he made money. As Philadelphia people figured wealth, he had become a rich man when he was forty-two years old. But money by itself did not interest him much. He had no taste for luxury. What he did value was the freedom that his comfortable income brought him to retire gradually from close attention to his business, freedom to spend his time on other things that seemed to him more worthwhile.

What sort of things were these? Here is a partial list. He always liked people and they liked him. He had already started the "Leather Apron Club," where a group of young wage earners came together in the evening after work to discuss and debate various subjects. Now he saw a way to give the club a more practical purpose. Each of its members owned a few books. Franklin suggested that these all might be stored for common use in the club room. Later the idea struck him that if everyone paid a small fee, more books could be bought. The plan worked, and grew into the first contribution library in America.

Again, he noticed that most of the houses in town were built of wood and some of them were always catching fire. Disorganized help from neighbors was of little use. So Franklin organized a fire-fighting company, equipped with leather buckets, called together by the ringing of church bells. Other companies were founded. Philadelphia's fire loss became so low that some years later the first Fire Insurance Company was set up. Naturally, B. Franklin was one of its directors. He also persuaded the city to pave its streets and light them with oil lanterns at night.

Winters were cold. People couldn't keep their houses warm. Franklin decided that the trouble came from the big fireplaces set deep into the walls. To get any heat at all you had to sit close to them and then, as the old saying went, "Your nose was roasted while the back of your neck was frozen." After he had thought the problem over, he drew some plans and hired an iron worker to make him a small metal fireplace connected to the chimney by a length of stove pipe. This contrivance stood so far out in a room that it threw off heat in every direction. He did not patent the invention. His idea was not to make money but to bring comfort to his fellow citizens, and he took care to rouse their interest by writing a clever advertising pamphlet which ended, "My living room, I know, is made twice as warm as it used to be, with a quarter of the wood I formerly consumed there."

All these activities were good. He thoroughly enjoyed himself as he took part in them. But what he really cared for most of all was science. His mind was always driving him to find answers to the question "What makes things act the way they do?" Just then, learned men were puzzled about electricity. They knew there was such a thing. They knew how to make a little of it by rubbing glass with silk. They were able to store it in a container which was like a very simple form of our automobile battery. They could make impressive sparks jump from wire to wire. That was the limit of what they could be sure about. Some of them wondered if perhaps this new substance was in some way connected with the lightning of a thunderstorm. It might be. But how could you prove it?

You know how Franklin did prove it, by coaxing some elec-

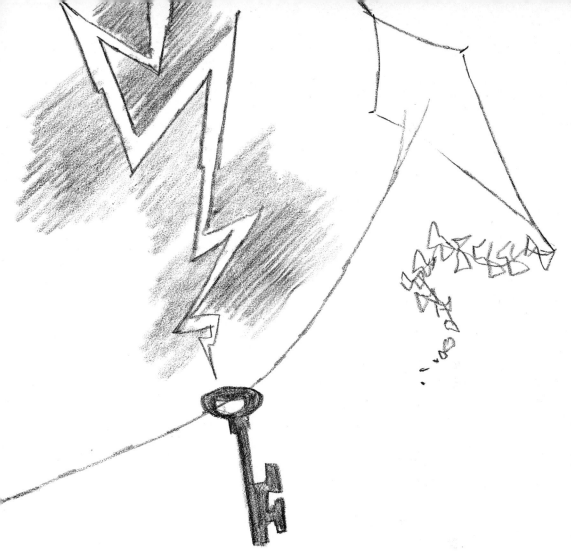

tricity down his kite string. From that time on he was a famous man both in America and Europe. But of course he did not stop there. All through his life, as soon as he learned any new fact, he wasn't satisfied until he had found a way to make that knowledge useful. "Why not put some metal spikes on top of your house?" he asked. "If you run wires from them down the outside of the wall and bury the lower end, won't the 'thunderbolt' slide harmlessly into the earth instead of burning your house?" People tried it. We are still using that principle in lightning rods. Once again he did not patent his invention. He was too busy trying to find out more about the way electricity acted to bother with making money out of it.

He learned a great deal more—so much that it seems incredible. His schooling had stopped when he was ten years old. He had only the simplest sort of testing apparatus to work with. Yet in a few years he had gone farther in this new branch of science than any university-trained scholar. He was patient, always ready to give up an attractive theory if the facts did not support it. More important still, something in his powerful mind led him to grasp his subject as a whole—to prove by one experiment after another the truth of general unchanging laws.

In the early days of his investigation, while he was still collecting facts and still more facts about *how* electricity acted, before he had any clear notions as to *why* it acted that way, he brought two wires from his lightning rod through the roof into his house until they hung in the open space beside the main stairway. He fastened a little bell to the end of each wire and waited for a thunderstorm. It came a night or two later. He was wakened by a loud crash, jumped out of bed and ran downstairs. Here is the way he described what he found: "The fire passed sometimes in very large quick cracks from bell to bell, and sometimes in a continued dense white stream, seemingly as large as my finger, whereby the whole staircase was inlighted as with sunshine, so that one might see to pick up a pin." What a charming picture! Can you see him as I imagine him, in a loose nightshirt, a red flannel nightcap on his head, sitting there on the bottom step, observing everything and thinking, thinking, thinking? Fortunately the storm was a light one, otherwise the fire department would have had a busy night. He doesn't tell us what the experience taught him. Probably the actual facts weren't important. The important part was what went on in that brain of his.

He would gladly have spent the rest of his days in quiet study and research. But he was now too prominent a figure to escape the responsibility of public service. First there was the French and Indian War, where he organized the supply train for the disastrous Braddock campaign. Later, although he knew nothing about military affairs, he somehow found himself in charge of the militia defending the western frontier. Finally, when peace was signed, friction began to grow acute between the Colonies and the British government.

Pennsylvania needed a strong agent to press its grievances before Parliament. Would Dr. Franklin accept the post? So he went to London and stayed there altogether over ten years. He got on splendidly with intelligent men of learning, received degrees from Oxford and St. Andrew's Universities, but he made very little impression on the King's ministers. He did his best and perhaps he delayed the crisis for a few years. These were the days of the Stamp Act and all the other turmoil of the period. At last, convinced that the feeling on both sides was too bitter for compromise, he came home just before the Revolutionary War started. In the Continental Congress he suggested a few minor changes in the wording of Jefferson's Declaration of Independence.

Again he was anxious to settle down in his comfortable home, and again it was the old story. He was drafted for a difficult mission. America needed money. It needed help of every kind to carry on the war, and who could better persuade France to give that help than the internationally respected Dr. Franklin? He was then a stout old man of seventy, in rather poor health; but he answered, "I am like a worn-out piece of carpet. If there is one corner left which can be useful to my country, I will be honored."

His first step was to turn over all the money he had on hand —between fifteen and twenty thousand dollars—as a loan to Congress for the purpose, as he put it, "of demonstrating his confidence, and encouraging others to lend their money also in support of the cause."

Then he went on board the sloop *Reprisal* and set sail across the Atlantic. No escort from the American Navy went along to guard him, for the excellent reason that, except for a few armed privateers, the American Navy did not exist. The six-weeks trip was perilous. By English law the Americans were rebels, and if captured, Franklin, as one of their notorious leaders, would certainly have been hanged for treason. What did he do to pass those days of helpless waiting for an attack which would have meant his death? Did he glue his eye to a spyglass and sweep the

horizon dreading to see a hostile sail? Not at all. He had been interested in the Gulf Stream ever since the captain of a Nantucket whaler had told him how much time could be saved by following that mysterious ocean current when sailing toward Europe, and avoiding it on the return trip. Here was Franklin's chance to make another contribution to knowledge by recording its exact location. Four or five times a day he dipped his thermometer in the water and entered the temperature on the chart. As the bald old gentleman bent over the railing to draw up his thermometer and make his observations he would have been astonished if anyone had told him that he was acting heroically. He took it for granted that as long as he had a teaspoonful of vitality left in him he would use it to help human life in the future to become safer, happier, and better than in the past. He would have said quite honestly that he was going on doing what he had always done—"just the best I can, whenever I have a chance. What's so heroic about that?"

He reached Paris rather bedraggled from his long voyage, and was astonished by the outburst of enthusiasm which greeted him. He was cheered by the crowds, invited to receptions and dinners by high society. Everyone seemed to know about his electrical discoveries, but that alone was not enough to account for his enormous popularity. He put his mind on the problem just as he had done when puzzled by something unexpected in his scientific experiments. For all his genuine simplicity of character he was a shrewd diplomat.

It took him only a few weeks to decide on the course most likely to win success for his mission. Among the higher nobility who had most influence with King Louis, there were two parties. One of these was ready to fight England at once. They hated the country which had beaten them in the last war and driven France out of Canada and India. The other party also hated England but they knew that the French finances were so badly strained that an all-out war might well bring bankruptcy. For the present then, Franklin could expect no more than secret loans of money and shipments of arms smuggled into the Colonies through the French West Indies. With such help Washington was just able to keep his armies in the field. He would need more before he could hope for final victory. Clearly Franklin's task was to influence the King by rousing more enthusiasm for America.

It was the fad, he found, to admire him as a philosopher from the backwoods—simple and unspoiled by decaying European civilization. Very well, if that was what they wanted from him, he would act the part. Writing to a friend he describes himself getting ready for a select dinner party: "Figure me in your mind very plainly dressed, wearing my thin gray straight hair that peeps out under my only coiffure, a fine fur cap, which comes down on my forehead almost to my spectacles. Think how this must appear among the powdered heads of Paris!" To all this he added his wonderful gift of finding just the right words, the right manner fitting to every occasion.

If the news from home was bad—as it often was—he never allowed himself to appear worried. He chatted cheerfully in his ungrammatical French. Everybody loved him, and in time even the most cautious of the King's advisors began to feel an affection for the people he represented, struggling against great odds for the right to govern themselves. He needed just one victory of American arms to conquer King Louis' hesitation. It came. Burgoyne's army surrendered at Saratoga. France signed a treaty of alliance with the Congress of the United States and declared war on England.

And that was a good thing for you and me. If it had not happened—who knows?—we might not have been born United States citizens. Only with the help of the French fleet, some years later, was Washington able to capture the army of Cornwallis at Yorktown, winning the war and independence.

As a very infirm old man, Franklin sat through the long tiresome sessions of our Constitutional Convention, and twice he used his great influence to bring about an agreement satisfying the quarrelsome delegates from both the big and the small states. In 1790 he died at the age of eighty-four.

His death was mourned everywhere. People quoted the translation of a Latin inscription on his statue in Paris: "He snatched lightning from the skies—and the scepter from the hands of a tyrant." But I don't think Franklin would have liked that. He was not vain. Such big words would have made him feel uncomfortable. Years before, in a letter to his mother, he had written out the only epitaph he wanted. He would be disappointed, he told her, if the best that could be said at his funeral would be, "He died a rich man." All he hoped for was that some of those who stood around his coffin would think:

"He led a useful life."

JOHN PAUL JONES

"I have not yet begun to fight."

John Paul Jones was one of those slam-bang boys, always taking a chance and getting away with it. Perhaps he was lucky—yes, sometimes he was. But there was more to it than luck.

John was born in 1747 in Scotland of hard-working and very poor parents named Paul. His father got a little pay for taking care of a rich man's garden. He also raised some food on a small plot of his own. That was not nearly enough to support a family, so most of the time he was a herring fisherman. This doesn't mean that he sat quietly, dropping his line from the end of a wharf, or walked along the bank of a stream with a fly rod. No, herring fishing was real work—hard, dangerous work. It meant putting out in a small open sailing boat from dawn till well into the night, battling with fierce winter gales on the North Sea, one of the most perilous corners of the ocean. A fisherman's son could never be sure that his father would get home safely. Many fathers never did come home.

So the boy who was afterward to fight so bravely in our Revolution spent his early years close to the shadow of death. It was from such a background that he absorbed through his pores the courage to face deadly danger without flinching.

At first little John Paul played and worked with his elder brother. But soon there was a change. A well-to-do Virginia plantation owner who was visiting Scotland took a fancy to William, offered to adopt him and bring him up in the new country as his own son. Mr. and Mrs. Paul did not let their feelings stand in the way of this splendid opportunity. William said good-bye and sailed away, leaving John Paul the oldest child at home.

When he was twelve years old, a shipowner from a port town to the south of Scotland came up into the region of hard-working fishermen and skillful sailors, hunting for a crew to man his new ship which had just been finished. He noticed some people standing on the beach looking out to sea and went down to find out what it was they were gazing at. It turned out to be a small fisherman's boat, which had been caught in a wind squall well out beyond the harbor and was now trying to get back to land. The boat was a yawl, which has more sails than one man can manage, and there were two figures in it as it came careening toward the rocks just outside the harbor. Mr. Younger, the shipbuilder and shipowner from England, could make out that one of the two appeared to be a little boy and the other a very old man. It was the little boy who seemed to be in command and who was managing the sails with a skill that made the shipowner rub his eyes. The yawl came in, leaning so far over as it sailed into the wind that one of the older men on the wharf exclaimed that the boy would never make it.

Another man said, "Yes, he will. He'll do it. He'll bring her in." Mr. Younger asked the second man, "Do you know that boy?"

The fisherman said, "Indeed I do. He's my son John. My name is Paul."

So Mr. Younger joined the watching group, and caught his breath in excitement as they did when the young sailor, with the ancient helper, came about just before dashing into the rocks, and went off again on a long tack almost out of sight. And then the yawl came back again on another tack. This one was evidently carefully calculated, for as the boat came nearer, the men on the wharf could see that there was just a chance that the young skipper could sail right through the narrow passage into the harbor without changing his course.

And so he did. Mr. Younger waited until the rosy youngster in charge of her came ashore. He was not large for his age but strong and well-muscled and perfectly composed.

Mr. Paul, the shabby fisherman, standing by the prosperous shipowner, said triumphantly, "I knew he could do it. He can sail anything."

Mr. Younger then and there signed on young John Paul to serve with him as captain's apprentice on the new ship just starting off from the British port. John Paul—only twelve years old—set to work with the tremendous energy of which he always had a large supply, to take advantage of this fresh opportunity to learn.

There were plenty of books on the difficult science and art of navigation in Captain Younger's library on the ship. And, since he was often in touch with French people in his trips here and there along the coast of France, John Paul studied French as hard as he studied navigation. Such a boy is always interesting to older men around him, and Captain Younger became convinced that the lad was of fine quality. By the time he was seventeen, he was advanced from captain's apprentice to the rank of second mate, and when he was eighteen he was made first mate.

Mr. Younger retired, released the nineteen-year-old lad from his apprentice's indentures, and made him a present of a one-eighth interest in a small packetboat on which the boy sailed as first mate. A year later, after two very profitable trading voyages, John Paul sold out his share in the boat and found himself with a thousand guineas (then about $5,000). This was quite a fortune for the twenty-year-old son of a very poor fisherman. From the West Indies he bought a ticket as a passenger on a ship going to England.

Whatever John Paul did turned out to be exciting. And this voyage was no exception. On the long, long trip across the Atlantic, all the officers and all but five of the sailors died of yellow fever. The young passenger who knew so well how to sail a ship was the only one available to take command. This he did, bring-

ing the vessel safely to the English port. It carried a cargo of con-
siderable value, and the owners, delighted with the young seaman's
skill and resolution, gave him 10 per cent of all the profits earned
on that trip and made him captain of a brand-new ship of theirs.

In this way he was able to visit Virginia and to meet again his
older brother William, who years before had been adopted by the
prosperous plantation owner Mr. Jones. The young captain made
such a favorable impression on old Mr. Jones that he added a
clause to his will, specifying that if his foster son William died without leaving heirs, young John Paul should inherit the plantation.
The old foster father died in 1760 and William died in 1763, leaving no heirs. So there was the young captain transformed into a
wealthy country gentleman. Something unexpected and fortunate
always seemed to happen to that John Paul. At this time he added
the name of old Mr. Jones to his. Who would have thought that
the son of the penniless Scottish fisherman would so soon have
plenty of money and be the owner of a lot of valuable land in North
America?

He was as generous and open-handed as he was lucky and attractive, and when the American Colonies began the Revolutionary
War to free themselves from England, the young Virginia planter
offered his services at once to Washington and Jefferson. They
both liked him on first sight. Most people did. As the man on
the American side who knew most about navigation, he took an
important part in getting a few ships armed and ready to put to sea.

This is why he is often called the Founder of the American Navy. He did so well with that job that he was sent on a mission to France, where old Ben Franklin was already busy at the French Court, representing the interests of the American Revolution. Franklin also took a great fancy to the short, vital young captain and was always his close friend.

After a time the young seaman was given a ship with which to attack the English navy. It was not a warship at all, but an old merchantman which had been used to take passengers and freight to India and back. It was not large and rather out of repair. John Paul called it the *Bonhomme Richard* after Franklin's "Poor Richard." John Paul Jones had, we have seen, plenty of energy. He did what he could to turn the ancient passenger ship into a fighting vessel, and although he knew very well that she was not going to break any records at sailing, she was the best he could get. So he set out with her to find out what she could do in a sea fight. It was in that fight—with a British man-of-war called the *Serapis*— that the young American commander shouted out a phrase which has never been forgotten by Americans. His words are as much part of our history as the name "Bunker Hill."

In this famous battle John Paul Jones had many things against him. He had a poor, old ship, hard to maneuver smartly, hastily refitted with cannons. He had a mixed-up crew. Some, but not many, were Americans; the rest were Oriental or French sailors. And as fighting force he had a small number of French marines, who couldn't be expected to feel much enthusiasm about risking their lives on the side of a new, poor country which hadn't even begun yet to exist as a nation. But as one of them said later, "Captain John could make a man brave by looking at him."

Against all these drawbacks he did have one advantage over his adversary. We must remember that in his time there was absolutely no way to move any ship an inch on the water except by taking advantage of the air currents. Captain John Paul Jones used to stand on the deck of his ship, his keen eyes fixed on the sails. He was studying them as he had studied navigation and French. Sometimes he took the wheel himself and changed the

52

course of the ship just a little, but precisely in the right direction so that sails, set at a new angle, caught a little more of the breeze and pushed his ship along, even in a quiet stillness that had other ships becalmed. His ship always seemed somehow to move into a better position. The sailors thought he had some magic power.

A whole convoy of merchant ships was coming down the English Channel, protected from attack by one small frigate and a heavily armed British man-of-war. Knowing that he had little chance in a long-range battle, Captain Jones at first dodged about here and there, then unexpectedly changed his tactics, steered straight on until he put his ancient East Indiaman just where he wanted to be—right alongside the larger of the enemy, the *Serapis*. The wind had gone down, the sea was still. The two vessels were so close to each other that those on the American decks could hear every word spoken by the British sailors. Only for a moment. Then pandemonium broke out as broadside answered thundering broadside.

The fire from the British cannon shook the old *Bonhomme Richard* from stem to stern, splintering decks and bulwarks, killing many of her crew. But with John Paul Jones' fiery eyes on them, the survivors fought back. The French gunners stuck to their posts. Americans loaded and fired their muskets, bringing down British sailors and marines with the accurate aim they had learned as boys, hunting wild game in the forest.

After an hour the commander of the *Serapis,* peering through thick smoke, was convinced that the battle was won. The old American ship seemed to him no more than a splintered, shattered wreck, actually on fire with flames shooting up wildly. And he thought he heard—so he testified later at court-martial—a shout coming from it begging for quarter, that is, surrendering.

Perhaps he was misled by the cry of some desperately wounded man, or in the clamor of the battle his ears may have deceived him. At any rate his own ship and crew had suffered so terribly that he welcomed an end to the slaughter. "Are you ready to give up?" he shouted through his speaking trumpet. The question rang loud above the tumult, and for an instant each bloodstained, powder-

blackened, grim fighting man halted where he stood to hear what the American captain would answer.

Then every one of them heard him shout back with an almost laughing defiance, "Surrender? Why, I have not yet begun to fight!"

His crew echoed his words with a cheer. They took courage from him—as we do—and fought on to victory.

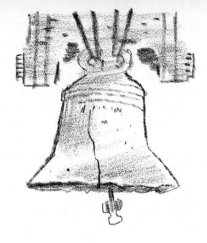

PATRICK HENRY

"Give me liberty or give me death!"

Once when we children were rummaging through old trunks in the storeroom, hunting for picturesque costumes to wear at a Halloween party, we came across an oddly shaped metal platter, carefully wrapped in a hand-woven linen sheet. It was colored a sort of dirty gray. We guessed it might be made of tin or pewter, and we couldn't imagine why anyone had bothered to put it away so carefully. Still, on the chance that it might remind some uncle or aunt of a story to tell us, we carried it downstairs—and then in the excitement of getting ready for the party, forgot all about it.

It was years later before I noticed that dingy piece of tableware again, perched on the back-pantry top shelf, where some tidal wave of spring house cleaning had left it stranded. Antiques were now in fashion. It occurred to me that the old plate or platter, or whatever it was, might turn out an interesting heirloom. So I lifted it down, washed and polished it carefully until I had rubbed off the tarnished outer coat. And there it was! . . . standing square on four claw-shaped feet, its rim delicately curved up, the glistening silver of its surface decorated with a faintly chased design. I made out a willow tree, a pagoda, obviously meant to suggest a scene in China. Why, of course, this must be a tea tray, probably the cherished wedding present of some eighteenth-century bride. I still treasure it, partly for its quaint charm, even more because just to look at it adds a breath of flesh-and-blood humanity to those shadowy figures—the actual men and women who lived through our country's first great age of decision. It's just a fancy, but I like to think the lady who owned that silver tray stopped using it at about the date of the famous Boston Tea Party.

I am sure that by this time you have made up your minds that I am not just rambling on about a pointless housekeeping incident. My tea tray, of course, is supposed to remind you that it is a good idea to look below the surface of familiar things. And I hope you will carry the idea a step further and see if it does not explain why history lessons often seem dull. If we merely skim over the pages, fixing our attention on a few disconnected facts likely to be useful in answering a "who said what . . . when?" examination, our reading can't help being dull. So was the outside of that antique tea tray of mine until I had curiosity enough to lay bare the precious metal so long hidden by surface tarnish.

I well remember once in school when we were annoyed by some faculty ruling—a shorter Christmas vacation than we expected, I think—how the class cut-up sent us into gales of laughter by shaking his clenched fist toward the closed door of the principal's office and declaiming, "Give me liberty, or give me death!" We thought those bombastic phrases were just too killingly funny. That's all we knew about it! Naturally, in our sheltered experience solemn words had lost their true meaning because we often used them in the effort to give dignity to our trivial hopes and fears.

In 1775, the delegates to the Virginia Convention had another scale of values. They were not, all of them, exactly clear as to what liberty meant. But they were positive about what it did not mean. They saw no liberty in the regulations laid down for them by the faraway Parliament at Westminster, strictly limiting the cargoes which American ships could carry and the ports to which they might sail; no liberty in the law forbidding any Colonist to make felt hats, iron or tinware, and various other manufactured objects—except for local use, *not* for shipment abroad. They were indignant at finding their westward expansion officially blocked by the Allegheny Mountains, at the high-handed suspension of Massachusetts' charter, at the British attempt to starve Boston into submission by a tight blockade allowing no ships to enter or leave the harbor. Above all they were outraged at having to pay any taxes, no matter how small, which had not been voted by their own elected legislatures.

Today, looking back across the eighteen decades which separate us from that hot quarrel, we can see that there was a good deal to be said on the other side. The British government was only following the usual eighteenth-century colonial policy. By the standards of that age it was not unduly rigging the game for the profit of the mother country, and friction did not necessarily mean the British Parliament's bad faith or vindictive motives. It simply could not carry out a satisfactory day-by-day, point-by-point government for an energetic, complex civilization three thousand miles away. Geography was against it! The ocean trip took at least six weeks, so that an official report asking directions for handling some difficulty was almost certain to be out of date when the answer finally reached the inquirer. During the three months of silent waiting there was plenty of time for some new and entirely different crisis to develop, raising popular discontent above the boiling point.

But the delegates to that Virginia Convention were in no mood to make allowances. They were sullen and out of patience with King George's "father knows best" autocratic rule. For colonies, like boys and girls, grow up, want to run their own lives, would rather make their own mistakes than be guided by even the best-intentioned parent. They all felt that some positive action must be taken. But what action?

Every eye was fixed on the well-known figure of Patrick Henry as he rose to present a resolution. Already he was the foremost courtroom lawyer in Virginia, had served in the House of Burgesses and in the First Continental Congress. Later in life he was to be elected Governor of the state five times, a member of its legislature as often as he chose, and to have the refusal of many important

Federal positions. But never in all his distinguished career did he rise to greater heights than on this momentous day.

His motion was that the militia should be armed, put on a war footing. Against what enemy? Against the combined sea and land power of Great Britain. That would be open rebellion, and the words now bluntly stated made everyone who heard him breathe deep and call to mind the outcome of an earlier rebellion, fought on British soil only thirty years before, to settle whether George II or Charles Edward Stuart should be King of England.

Don't be surprised by that word "only." To the young, naturally enough, whatever takes place before they were born seems incredibly remote. But to elderly or middle-aged people (as those delegates were) the memories roused by a flashback of thirty years are as vivid as those of the day before yesterday. Besides, what had happened in 1745 was not easy to forget. The rebellion had been crushed. Then, after the fighting was finished, more than fifty of the most prominent on the losing side had been executed in cold blood, suffering the long-drawn-out agony decreed by a ferocious criminal code as punishment for high treason.

Everybody knew the story. It was no secret. On the contrary, all the ghastly details had been broadcast as a warning of the bitter last chapter to be expected by future rebels against His Gracious Majesty the King.

One cannot possibly understand this country's history if it is supposed that in the eighteenth century setting up a new government was as simple and safe, as much a matter of free personal choice as it would be for people to switch their political parties at the next election. Oh yes, a limited group of Colonial citizens had votes on minor local issues, but in 1775 when the government gave orders, its subjects obeyed, or else. . . .

The shadow of that threatening "or else" hung darkest over men in the front rank. John Hancock, Benjamin Franklin, John and Samuel Adams, George Washington, and many more—each of them must have known that if the hastily mustered Minutemen broke before the seasoned Redcoats, his own life could end either in a prison cell or on the scaffold.

To be sure, George III might be more lenient than his father. The majority of ordinary workers in the movement who had not made themselves too conspicuous could reasonably hope for pardons. But not the outstanding leaders. Open resistance to the King was still treason. The penalty for treason had not been changed.

Among the patriots who saw with clear eyes the grim risk they were taking, and yet walked steadily forward toward whatever the future might bring, Patrick Henry stands high. He was one of the first to call for all-out revolt in language so plain it could not be misunderstood, before a public assembly where everything he said was noted and recorded. Urging the passage of his motion by the Virginia Convention that day in 1775 (remember that no concerted policy among the thirteen Colonies had yet been agreed on—the Declaration of Independence was not signed until July in the following year), he pointed out that arguments and petitions had been tried all through the past ten years. They always had

failed and always would fail. Why were new troops constantly added to the British garrison at Boston? Clearly they were being sent there to enforce obedience. Delay would be fatal. Since there was no other choice, force must be met by force before it was too late. "Gentlemen," he cried, "we must fight. I repeat it, *We must fight!*" He was no cheap actor playing tricks on his audience with empty rhetoric. He meant exactly what he said. He was speaking out his deepest convictions when he came to his great climax: "Is life so dear, or peace so sweet as to be purchased at the price of chains and slavery? Forbid it, Almighty God! I know not what course others may take, but as for me, give me *liberty*, or give me death!"

Those words, ringing clear as a bugle call sounding the charge, rallied the waverers and swept Virginia forward into the eight-year desperate struggle of the Revolution . . . to final peace under a new national flag, the red, white, and blue of the United States.

NATHAN HALE

". . . every kind of service necessary to the public good becomes honorable by being necessary."

Just look around your group and pick out the boy who is usually thought to be the one "surest to succeed in life." That's the kind of a boy Nathan Hale was. That is, if the boy you have chosen is big and strong, good-looking, a good sport, loving outdoor games and hunting and fishing, full of fun, good at his books, and life-enjoying. Nathan Hale was all this—and he was also very fortunate in his family.

I don't mean that his folks had a lot of money and didn't have to work. Just the other way. The original Hale who came to this country early in the 1630s was a blacksmith by trade. But he was also a deacon in the church, and a selectman of the town (that's quite an honor). He owned land and sent his oldest son to Harvard. That's the way the Hales began life in America, and so they continued, Harvard graduates and farmers, professional men and working people, for a century and a quarter, till 1755. That's when Nathan Hale was born. By this time some of the Hales lived in western Connecticut, near Hartford, where, as early as anywhere in the Colonies, people felt themselves to be Americans, not British.

It was a Hale tradition that their sons should be well-educated, so when Nathan Hale and his brother were old enough they were sent to the nearest college. This was Yale. It was not much more than a high school at that time; Nathan's class had only thirty-six in it, and there were about a hundred in the whole school. But it was a very good high school, where Greek, Latin, and even some Hebrew, logic, rhetoric, and geometry were studied. But apparently the favorite of the students was debating. There was a lot of lively give-and-take in these debates, not only about the ideas they were discussing, but about the grammar and the choice of words used by the boys on the platform. They got the hang of making fine expressions for their best ideas. You could have guessed this from the noble phrase which is the great gift Nathan Hale left for us all.

The commencement of the Class of 1773 lasted all day! Part of the program was a debate between Nathan Hale and some other students on this question: "Whether the education of Daughters be not without any just reason more neglected than that of Sons." It was one of Nathan Hale's special ideas that girls as well as boys should be educated. He kept it in his mind alongside another radical, revolutionary notion—the idea that American Colonists should be free to develop all their powers, as only independence allows people to grow. Why, he asked, shouldn't girls be allowed to grow into mature strength and power of personality as much as boys?

When he left Yale, he began to teach. The six-foot-tall, handsome, strong, active, intelligent, outdoor fellow was a success as an educator. And, alongside his school for boys, he opened a class for girls. He lived up to his ideals, you see—he always did. The only time available was very early in the morning before he began his work at the school for boys. So he and the class of girls began their studies at five in the morning, and ended at seven. But the tall, powerful young schoolmaster found these long hours no hardship. He never found anything a hardship which seemed to him worth doing. He had practically decided that he would make teaching his lifework, because he enjoyed it so much.

But as 1776 came in, he soon saw that his lifework was not to be teaching, at least not just yet. In the years between 1773 (when Nathan Hale began to teach) and 1775, public meetings and debates were fairly boiling with discussions about the possibility of winning independence from Great Britain. Nathan Hale had been using in public speaking all the skill he had learned at Yale, putting his heart into the arguments for American independence.

He went enthusiastically into the American Army. He studied military affairs as hard as he had his Yale lessons. And he trained the men under him just as skillfully as he had taught school. By January, 1776, he was a full captain; and in March, with a well-trained body of men and, so he wrote a friend, "five days' cooked rations," he started for Long Island. At the same time, he wrote to his family, "It gives pleasure to every friend of his country to observe the health which prevails in our army. The army is every day improving in discipline, and it is hoped will soon be able to meet the enemy at any kind of play." His men were as full of good spirits as he. All young, with a commander whom they respected and liked, they set off as on a great adventure.

But schoolmasters, no matter how able and much loved by their men, cannot with a few weeks' drill change farmers and shop keepers into an army of real soldiers, who will be able to turn back seasoned professionals. What happened to them in the first contact with the British troops? Just take a look at American history, and you'll find that the Colonials had a terrible experience of defeat—with 1,100 men lost or captured. Nathan Hale saw many comrades of his school and boyhood days killed, or heard that they had been captured. But it was not a complete disaster, for a large number were able to get across to the city of New York.

It was his first experience with the blackness of defeat. This is the way he took it. It was necessary to know, if possible, when and where the British Army would cross the East River and get into New York, to which the Americans had now retreated. Nathan Hale volunteered to go into the British camp and try to find out the number of men there, how the regiments were grouped, and what their plans were. He wrote, "I am fully aware of the con-

sequences of being discovered and captured. I wish to be useful
and *every kind of service necessary to the public good becomes
honorable by being necessary."* This in a hastily written personal
letter. His practice in debating had made him skillful in the use
of words to express his ideas.

So, in plain clothes, looking like a civilian, and saying (truth-
fully enough) that he was a schoolmaster, he went into the British
camp.

He was captured. Drawings and memoranda about the
British camp were found in his shoes where he had hidden them.

After that, not a word. As far as his family and friends knew,
he seemed to have stepped off the edge of the world into nothing-
ness.

But his brothers and many of his comrades in the American
Army were not content to lose all trace of him. They set to work
to find out what had happened. It did not take long. Every day
forage detachments went out from the British camp into the
countryside to gather provisions. They spoke freely with the Long
Island farmers who, no matter what their sympathies might be,
had not yet taken up arms, and were therefore treated as harmless

noncombatants. Soon one of these farmers sent a smuggled message through. Yes, he had got this information from soldiers who had been on guard duty on September 21. That evening the prisoner had written several letters. (Knowing the kind of a man he was, we can be sure he would have wanted to get word back to his friends and the girl he was going to marry.) But an officer had torn those letters up and thrown them away. The very next morning after he had been captured, the prisoner had been hanged— as a spy.

Well, he was a spy. He knew exactly the risk he was taking. And he had been willing to take that risk.

Once when I was telling this story to a friend of mine he interrupted me impatiently: "I don't understand why you make such a fuss about this man Hale. All I see in it is that he was a failure. He didn't get back with the information Washington needed."

I thought, and still think, that friend extremely narrow-minded. Let's consider the matter in the way Nathan and his classmates used to argue together at Yale. This is the question: "What do we mean by success in life?" Isn't it to be honest, kind, and brave, to follow the truth as we see it, to care less for our own comfort than for the good of others? And do we think a life so lived is a failure, not worth remembering, because through lack of caution or a stroke of bad luck, a single mission was not accomplished? No. No. No! It won't do! I can't write a dispassionate outline of the arguments for both sides of the question because, no matter how I try, I can see only one side to it. Even my hard-boiled critic might have agreed with me if he had waited to hear the end of my story. For there is more to it.

Nathan Hale did not bring back the enemy's plans to Washington. But he did send something more important—a rallying cry to all America.

This his friends learned from another British soldier who had been present at his execution. A military band had been drawn up at the foot of the scaffold. They had orders to drown out with a thundering roll of drums anything the prisoner might say. This they did, their sticks flying on the drumheads, as Nathan Hale, tall, vital, young, was marched, his hands tied behind his back, to the foot of the platform and then up the steps.

But at the moment when the noose was dropped around his neck, there was a pause—a moment's silence.

Nathan Hale was ready. In a quiet, clear voice he said, "My only regret is that I have but one life to give for my country"— and died.

You may become famous, rich, much loved, and happy in the long life that lies before you.

But not one of you will ever have a more successful life than Nathan Hale.

DAVID FARRAGUT

"Never mind the danger!   Full speed ahead!"

It couldn't be said that David Farragut was born, brought up, and lived his life out on a ship.   But almost. His father too was a man of the sea, for he came as a shipmaster to New Orleans from Minorca, a little island in the Mediterranean. And his foster father was the great Admiral Porter, a naval hero of the War of 1812.

Most boys nine years old play tag and go skating.   When Farragut was that age—it was in 1810—he was midshipman on an American battleship.   It seemed as natural to him as playing tag. He was small, as lively and active as a monkey, cheerful, full of fun, with good brains for learning.

And that's the kind of man he was when he grew up and became an officer in the American Navy.   He was a good navigator, managed his crew as well as his ship, enjoyed life, and saw to it that the people around him did.   If the Civil War hadn't broken out, we probably would never have known anything more about him. But it did break out.

He was an elderly man, past sixty, when in 1861 the American flag was fired on at Fort Sumter, and officers serving the Federal government had to decide which side they would fight on.   It didn't take Farragut a minute to decide that he would fight for the Union.

And it was in the course of that war that this gray-haired little man with the lion's heart gave us two examples of bravery—one cool, resolute, and enduring, the other hot, reckless as a flame. The memory of both of them ever since has helped Americans when they found themselves in a tight place.

In one fierce naval battle, he climbed up on the mast of his flagship and tied himself there (so he could have both hands free to hold his telescope) right in the middle of the flying shells and shots, shouting down his commands to his sailors and gunners. If the ship had been sunk, he would have gone down with her. Any bullet might have killed him instantly. But there he perched, his gray hair flying, his old face keen, intent, composed, doing what had to be done, till victory was won.

How many times, I wonder, has an American girl telephone operator at the switchboard of a city threatened by a flood, or an American fireman in a dangerous place, holding a hose to fight flames, thought of the cool steady bravery of the gray-haired old admiral—and stood fast, as Farragut did?

The other reason why Farragut has not been forgotten by Americans of all ages is not quiet and steady. The memory flares up, and in its sudden light many an American has plunged recklessly forward to do what had to be done, even when it seemed impossible.

It was at the beginning of the Battle of Mobile Bay. He was on the flagship. Ahead of him was a big American Navy battleship, the *Brooklyn,* and several monitors (small, iron-clad boats with big cannon). They were all advancing into a channel strongly defended by a heavily armored battleship and a fort, as well as by torpedoes and mines, thickly strewn on the water and ready to explode at a touch.

As they advanced, one of the monitors grazed a mine. Like a volcano erupting, the mine went off and flung the monitor right out of the water, blowing the boat and the men on her into a thousand fragments. The *Brooklyn* stopped short, its captain not knowing what to do. There was an awful pause when nobody knew what to do.

And in that moment, the tide began to carry the halted monitors and battleships right toward the fort with its threatening cannon. If that terrible halt had lasted another moment there would have been a tragic disaster. But it did not last.

On the flagship old David Farragut exploded into a fury of courage. He cried out an order which in threatened disaster has carried Americans forward ever since. "Damn the torpedoes!" he shouted. "Full speed ahead!"

The ships, the monitors, moved ahead. The floating mines could be heard scraping against their hulls. But none exploded. The danger was passed. The battle was won.

It is nearly a century since that wild blaze of courage flared up in an old man's heart. But it has blazed up again ever since, when Americans trying to do something they knew they ought to do found themselves blocked by a deadly danger.

Leading from the past, old Admiral Farragut has shouted to them, "Never mind the danger! Full speed ahead!"

And they've gone ahead.

DOROTHEA DIX

The most precious gift is our share of the power to grow.

In your school work when you got beyond reciting "nine times twelve is one hundred and eight," and began to use arithmetic in solving problems, did some teasing older person ever ask you solemnly, "What happens when an irresistible force meets an immovable object?" And as you grew older did you perhaps try to get even for having been teased by passing the bewildering problem on to a younger child? The catch about it is, of course, that stated in the abstract as it is, no solution is possible. Also it is a bit foolish, because those big sweeping words in it never exactly fit the facts of the real world. Sometimes, I admit, in our actual daily experience objects do *seem* immovable and forces irresistible. When they meet, what happens? Well, let's see what did happen in the life of Dorothea Dix.

She was born in Maine in the year 1802. Her father was a ne'er-do-well who loafed and drank and provided the most miserable of homes, a tumbledown log cabin in the woods, for his wife and family of small children. His little girl, she who was to become the irresistible force, didn't look much like it then. As she struggled through the snowbanks back to the cabin lugging an iron kettle full of spring water, or choked with smoke as she cooked meals over the open hearth fire, no one could have guessed that she herself was to become a flame of power for righteousness.

Even after she was twelve years old, when her grandmother sent for her to come down to Boston to study to become a schoolteacher so that she could earn her own living, she didn't look as though she would ever do very much in the world. She was a sickly, pale little girl when she made that journey and went to live with her grandmother, who was the widow of a well-to-do man, living in idleness by herself with a faithful household staff of helpers. Little Dorothea was not very attractive, and her grandmother didn't take to her at all. Nor did anybody else especially. But Dorothea realized fully that this was the best chance she would ever have to get out of the black hole into which her father's shiftlessness had plunged her, and she set to work with fierce energy to learn what was necessary (not so very much, I imagine) to teach school for girls. In those days girls were not supposed to learn very much, or to know very much.

All this time Dorothea's grandmother paid no attention to what happened to the girl, except to give her meals and a bed to sleep on. So the child was as alone in life as if she had no relatives.

When she was fourteen years old she was given a trial at teaching a class of young children (something like what we would now call a kindergarten, I think). She showed enough promise as a teacher to induce her grandmother to go on paying for her tuition in the other subjects she would need later. After a while she had learned enough to be ready to begin the real teaching which she and her relatives thought was to be her lifework.

She was nineteen years old now, and frail in health as she always had been. But since she wasn't actually sick in bed, nobody told her to go slow and take a rest. Her grandmother's comfortable house was very grim. Not a word of tenderness was spoken there. But Dorothea had never known loving care anywhere. So she set her teeth and just plunged ahead, trying to find a way to start a life of her own. For, of course, she hadn't a penny and knew that she would have to depend entirely on her own efforts. Above all, she made up her mind desperately never to be a burden on anybody.

Her school for young ladies was a success. It was one of the first reasonably serious schools for girls on the North American continent. She worked at it with a dreadful tenseness of anxiety lest she should fail. And by 1835, when she was thirty-three years old, she had worked herself into a complete breakdown in health.

A doctor examined her and reported that she would never again be well enough to teach. This meant despair for Dorothea and bleak disapproval on the part of her grandmother. He also suggested that the change of air from a sea trip "might be beneficial."

Doctors often prescribed a change of air when they couldn't think of anything else to say. Desolate and defeated, sure that she had come to the end of her life, she set sail for England in the spring of 1836 and stayed eighteen months near Liverpool at the home of friends of her family, people who had never known her before. But she was not shy of strangers after such a period of fighting her way in the world, and in this English home she found an atmosphere of warm, affectionate companionship and family feeling that she had never known before. Astonished by discovering that life need not always be dark and cold and severe, she blossomed.

You must have seen at some time a wild grape vine coming to life as the ground thaws, and not doing very well, just managing to keep alive. After a spell of good spring weather with warm sun and plenty of rain, all of a sudden a green shoot starts up from its brown woody tip and stands there wavering to and fro uncertainly, as if hunting for some support on which to grow higher. It looks weak, and it is. You could break it between your fingers.

But when it does find a support, how it does grow, up and up, wrapping its tendrils round and round any stiff hardwood sapling within reach. And as it grows up, it grows strong—so strong, with such tough fibres, that the heaviest man can swing on it without its breaking. That's one of the miracles of growth. Dorothea Dix's life was another such miracle.

When Dorothea got back to Boston after her first and only experience of good growing weather, no one could have guessed that in her personality a green living shoot was ready to burst from its bud sheath out into the air and sunlight. As she walked along the street passers-by saw her only as a rather feeble, ugly old maid. That's the way she saw herself reflected in her dressing-room looking glass.

It was in 1837 that she came back from England, and that very year the unloving old grandmother died. Dorothea, her sickly granddaughter was heir to the house and an income of $3,000 a year, which was considered a lot of money in those days. Although this may sound like a made-up fairy tale, that's the way it happened. My guess is that when the old lady made her will, she secretly admired her granddaughter's spunk in doing her best to stand up against difficulties. But of course she was such a repressed individual that she would have felt ashamed to speak right out and put such a mushy feeling into words.

Dorothea's doctor found her much better, and laid it to the "change of air." I think it very probable that a house of her own and an independent income had a great deal to do with her pick-up in health. Then it was that Dorothea Dix must have supposed she was settled in life and from that minute on would find nothing else to do but fold her shawl around her thin shoulders and be an elderly invalid, interested only in taking care of herself. Nothing more was expected of such women . . . when they could afford it.

About this time a young student in a theological seminary wanted to do what was expected of him, and that was to carry on church work among the poor and needy. It seemed to him that the best way to do that was to start a Sunday school in the Cambridge jail, just across the river from Boston. On his first trip there he saw that there were some women among these prisoners, and in those days it was not thought proper for a man to be alone with a group of women pupils. So he cast his eyes around to find a respectable lady who might be willing to give Sunday-school lessons. His mother suggested Miss Dorothea Dix. Such an errand was exactly suitable for a homely, respectable old maid living alone. "Yes," Miss Dix told the young theological student, she would do it. Next morning she put on her shawl and her warm overshoes because there was snow on the ground, and by agreement met the young theological student at the Cambridge jail. She was all prepared to teach the women Sunday-school lessons for an hour and then go back to her comfortable home. But what she found inside the jail set her heart to burning with pity and horror and the impulse to help misery.

For behind the prisoners she saw a wretched group of people in a room without a particle of fire, although there was a stove in it—an empty stove. They were freezingly cold, barefooted, in rags. She asked the jailer, with the authority of an old schoolteacher, why there was no fire burning. He answered at once, repeating what everybody thought at that time, "Oh, the people in there are lunatics, and loonies don't feel the cold."

The slender green shoot of Dorothea's character stopped waving to and fro. Its tendril wrapped itself tightly around the idea of giving help where it was needed, to the helpless, to the hopeless.

Back in Boston she could not rest until she had thought of a way to get a fire lighted in that stove. After a while she came up with a plan which only a schoolteacher would have thought of. Experience had taught her that unruly pupils could be made to behave themselves if she told them what they ought to do in a firm, loud voice. So she wrote a firm, positive letter to the officers of the court in East Cambridge, describing the shocking situation in the jail under their jurisdiction and asking them—almost ordering them—to *do something about it at once*. In turn, the Honorable Court firmly and positively directed the jailer to keep that room warm. Of course he did what they told him to. The fire was lighted . . . the room kept warm.

After her first victory, Dorothea grew some more. Was it possible, she wondered, that in other places there was the same suffering she had found at Cambridge? Yes, that was likely . . . now another tendril gripped a stout conviction . . . but no matter how frightful the need might be, *she could help*.

What's the use of trying to describe the inner workings of a miracle? All I can do is just to go on telling you what happened. The story is history, with all the documents needed to prove that it really did take place. Miss Dix now began to go about in the Massachusetts countryside to see for herself how insane people were treated. She found conditions always bad, sometimes so terrible that she hardly dared speak of them to other ladies, because "ladies" were not supposed to know about disgusting conditions of any kind. She found, for instance, that the jailer's ideas were accepted everywhere. Lunatics couldn't feel the cold, wouldn't understand being treated kindly. Some families kept their insane at home, locked up alone in an unheated attic room, fed with left-over scraps, often filthy and shivering in the cruelly cold New England winter.

It was not only inside the Cambridge jail that a fire was lighted. Another fire burned hot in the heart and soul—above all in the imagination of the plain, orderly, retired schoolteacher. Space and time vanished, as her indignation flared up, throwing its light farther and farther around her country. If mentally deranged people were so treated in Massachusetts, her home state, what was going on in other states?

She went to Rhode Island and asked questions, looking as she always had looked, elderly, plain, very ladylike in her manner. But the fire kindled within made itself felt wherever she went. Nobody could turn away when she denounced the outrage of treating human beings who had done no wrong thing more savagely than the wickedest criminals. She found conditions in Rhode Island just as they were in Massachusetts. No, not quite. There really was a lunatic hospital at Providence, built and meagerly maintained by charity, where the insane were kept as well (at least) as horses or pigs, with a roof over their heads so that they did not have to lie down and die in the streets. But so small! Only a few of the many who needed refuge could be taken in. "How much money would it take to make it larger?" she asked.

"That's out of the question," she was told. "Forty thousand

dollars . . . too much to hope for. Nobody but Mr. Butler has that kind of money, and he would never give a penny."

So Dorothea Dix went to see Mr. Butler in his large handsome house. No servant would refuse to admit a *lady,* not young, not robust, very quiet in manner, who asked to see Mr. Butler for a short interview. He tried to put her off by talking about the weather, but soon she was telling him in her quiet way some of the horrible things being done to harmless men and women within hearing of his fine house. Like everybody else who heard her thus speak of what she herself had seen, he listened as if hypnotized . . . as if a spell had been cast over him. When she drew breath, he asked, "What do you expect *me* to do about all this?"

She answered, "Give forty thousand dollars to enlarge the lunatic hospital."

He answered like a man talking in his sleep, "I'll do it."

With this promise she went away, the inner fire burning more hotly than ever with new fuel of *hope in human nature.* For remember this true story had two great elements in it. Not only the woman burning like a flame with horror and pity, but the men and women everywhere who listened as she spoke . . . who felt shame at their former blindness to the great need . . . who, once they had heard the story from her own lips, stepped forward to help—not her, but the wretched sufferers for whom she pleaded.

She carried her one-woman crusade on into New Jersey, where there had been no provision whatever for the mentally deranged. The legislature was in session. She was careful not to overstep the limits of what was then considered decorous. She did not ask permission to make a public address. That was not necessary, for already she was so much respected that a room was set aside for her in the library, where, in ladylike seclusion, she could receive any legislator willing to hear her story. Once they stepped in they were lost. Again, she simply told them what she had seen of the frightful sufferings of the mentally unbalanced in their own state, in many cases in their own towns.

A bill was promptly introduced to set up a state asylum. This was the first attempt to create such an asylum with tax money, and you must not think it was done without opposition. Rock-ribbed conservatives shook their fists and shouted, "Stop! Look! Listen! Think what it will cost!" One member, during the assembly debate said, "New Jersey has hitherto acted well. The state has kept clear of the national debt. I do believe this—if Miss Dix had been paid five or six hundred dollars and escorted over the border to Delaware or to Philadelphia, or even one thousand dollars and taken to Washington . . . it would have been money well laid out."

When the measure came up before the legislature, he was voted down and enough money appropriated to provide for the asylum. This was on March 25, 1845.

The work went on. At the end of that year, Dorothea wrote a private report to Mrs. Rathbone, the English lady in whose home she had spent the only personally happy months of her life. It ran: "Traveled over 10,000 miles in three years, visited 18 Peni-

tentiaries, 300 County Jails, etc., 500 alms-houses and other institutions besides hospitals and houses of refuge. Established 6 hospitals for insane, several County poor houses, several jails on the reform plan." Alone, she had traveled all those miles from Nova Scotia to New Orleans and back. Alone, she had visited the insane wherever she found them in any of the states along the way. This in a time when for a woman to mingle with strangers was taken as proof that she could not be a lady. But nobody any longer thought of applying such rules to Miss Dix. She had become herself an institution.

It's hard to realize what such a trip meant. Over rough, rutted, frozen roads she drove, from small unheated way stations along her railroad trips. She traveled these perhaps with a farmer driving the horses, someone quite unknown to her, to the barn or the cellar or the outhouse where she had heard of some insane person locked up in custody.

She carried her reforms through the legislatures of Illinois, Kentucky, Tennessee, Missouri, Mississippi, Louisiana, Alabama, South Carolina, North Carolina, Maryland, Halifax, Nova Scotia, St. Johns, Newfoundland.

She was seventy-seven years old when her health finally gave way. Think of it! In her early thirties the doctor had predicted for her only a few secluded years as a semi-invalid. Only now, forty-four years later, did she cease driving herself steadily, tirelessly, supervising the treatment given in the asylums she had brought into being. She spent her last years in one of them. By that date New Jersey had a fine stately building for the care of the insane, surrounded by beautiful flowering shrubs and broad-branching trees. There, by a vote of the board of trustees, she was given a comfortable room and cared for during the long years of her last illness. When at last she died she was eighty-five years old. The sickly little girl from Maine had climbed high, hadn't she, on the support of a lofty ideal . . . forgetting her own welfare, forgetting herself, passionately trying to do her best for the most helpless and the most terribly suffering human beings she knew.

What was the immovable object in this story? It was human nature. Many people believe that when an old prejudice gets firmly fixed in the general mind of humanity, nothing can be done about it. But this strange and true and beautiful story proves that nothing ever is—or can be—immovable. While human nature is made up of all kinds of things, good and bad, there is always good enough mixed with its bad so that when a noble cause finds a great leader, the good in humanity cannot hang back. It must conquer the bad and start growth toward the better.

The story of Dorothea Dix and her adventure with the human race is the story of the growth of both of them.

All growth is a miracle that nobody can really understand but, slow or fast, it keeps going on everywhere, all the time. The most precious gift we are born with is our share of the power to grow.

ROBERT E. LEE

"Boys go home and . . . build up what has been broken by the war . . ."

We hear people say that nobody—man, woman, boy, or girl—can know what is going to happen in life. True enough! We can't be positive about definite facts, about what we will be doing or where we will be living next year—or even next week. But some things are so very, very likely to happen in anyone's life that it is wise to expect them and try to prepare for them in ours. Through the years ahead, for instance, there isn't one chance in ten thousand that our side is going to win every game, every debate, every contest. Not one of us is *always* going to come out on top.

How are we going to take defeat when it happens? Will we be good losers or bad ones? There are two ways of being a bad loser. Both of them are worse than useless. One way is to laugh off our failures—to tell ourselves that it really doesn't matter, that nothing ever is worth caring about, so we won't try any more, just let life slide along as it happens. The other way is to blow up, to get so furious at not winning that you don't want anything to go right. When somebody on the losing side hates all the people on the winning side, of course what he'd really like is to have everything go wrong from that minute. That kind of loser can't possibly put his mind on trying to think what's the best thing to do next.

But something must always be done next.

It's up to everybody, winner and loser, to help make the next thing done the right thing.

We couldn't have a finer example of that good way to take losing than the way General Lee took after his side lost.

General Lee had been fighting bravely, with all his heart, for what he thought was the Good Cause. What was that cause? He was not at all one of those who were fighting to keep Negro men, women, and children enslaved. He himself did not own any slaves, and five years before the Civil War broke out, General Lee had written to a friend: "There are few, I believe, but will acknowledge that slavery is a moral and political evil in any country. I think it a greater evil to the white race than to the black race."

No, it was not slavery which made General Lee join the Confederate Army. It was something else—something he cared about intensely—with all his heart. Although it seemed terrible to him to resign from the United States Army, in which he had served proudly so many years as an officer, he felt that now he had no other choice. He was a Virginian, first of all. A citizen's deepest duty, as he saw it, is loyalty to the state where he was born. Virginia was his home. When an army made up of men from other states threatened to invade Virginia, how could a loyal son hesitate to join in defence of his mother land?

At that time a great many honorable, patriotic men saw the problem as Lee did. But that was nearly a hundred years ago. The United States could never have taken its place among the nations of the world if its government could not speak for all its people . . . if it represented no more than a loosely organized alliance of sovereign states, so independent that they could at any time decide to remain in the Union or drop out of it.

But though we may think that in the great crisis of 1861 Robert E. Lee made a mistake of judgment, none of us can doubt that he acted from an honest conviction of his duty. In all his life he never did a single thing he thought morally wrong.

Lee was a very gifted general, and a very brave man. He kept up the war effort just as long as it was possible to hope for success in it. But his side was beaten. The South just couldn't go on any longer. General Lee met with General Grant at a little place called Appomattox and there admitted the total defeat of the South. It was a terrible blow to General Lee. He took it in a noble way; at once he set his mind to think what was the best thing to do next.

Of course, ever so many other people in the Confederate Army of the South were defeated at the same time. Not all of them took it as grandly as General Lee did. Some were so angry that they went to live outside the United States. For instance, some became officers in the Egyptian Army. Some went to Mexico to work for the Mexican government. Some went to South America to bring up their children away from the spot where their idea of how to manage life had been beaten.

But most of them, after they had taken a little time to get over the bitterest part of their disappointment, set out bravely to earn their livings and support their families by working. Many Southern officers were West Point graduates and had learned how to build bridges and make roads. Of these, many devoted themselves to improving transportation in the South. Others worked the land in the country, went into business in towns, set up factories to make what was needed in everyday life. It is fair to say that the reason why so many of them had the courage and endurance to start life all over again and work their way up from the very bottom in their desperately war-wasted country can be found in the example set them by General Lee.

Just what was that example? For most Americans, the last sight of Robert E. Lee is as the history books describe him. This is after his surrender to General Grant at Appomattox. He rides away from the little house where he had just admitted total defeat, a stately figure on his famous white horse Traveller, dressed in a fine, pearl-gray uniform with a red silk sash.

But that wasn't the way he looked the next day when, in a worn old uniform, he and Traveller, both of them splashed with mud, went soberly back to everyday life, to the responsibility of earning his living and that of his two daughters and his wife, a wheel-chair invalid. His outer aspect at that moment wasn't so glorious, but from that minute on his life was of glorious value to us all. Without losing an ounce of strength or a minute of time in pitying himself because his side had lost, he used all he had to open the door to the future for young Americans. That was, he saw, the next thing that was needed by his country. That was what he did.

Famous, admired, beloved by hundreds of thousands of his countrymen, Lee found that wherever he went the crowds of admiring spectators were almost mobs in size. They always cheered and shouted for him. But he didn't spend much time appearing in public as the subject of all this admiration. He stayed put, and worked quietly all the rest of his life to build up a small, poor, little-known college. He had accepted the offer of the presidency of Washington College, which had at that time few students and almost no money in its treasury. It was named for George Washington, who had helped it in the last years of his life. General Lee's salary was to be $125 a month, a house in pretty bad condition, and a garden. There were a hundred and forty-six students, fifty-nine of them from outside Virginia. The tuition was $75 a year. The treasurer had on hand a little over $2,000 in Confederate money—and that meant almost nothing in real cash.

What Lee was too modest to see was, of course, that just his going there was an enormous help. People who had never heard of the college became interested. Rich people began to make contributions. New students came to it. Two years after he went there the number of students had more than doubled and there was real money in the treasury. Lee settled down to use his best thought to make the education there the most useful to the young men of the South.

He was then fifty-eight years old, and naturally his college education was far in the past. It had been the old-fashioned kind with plenty of book-learning. Book-learning being natural to him, Washington College had plenty of it—Latin, Greek, mathematics, philosophy, English, modern history, and so on. But under Lee's guidance, it also had what was newer in college education then— fine courses in science, chemistry and physics; and—almost unknown then in colleges—a practical course in agriculture. And he proposed a subject then unheard of in higher education—a course in journalism. He himself knew nothing about newspaper work, but he said, "Printing is one of the arts that diffuse education. We should seek, therefore, to qualify printers for the task of educating, to make them better and more cultured editors." It was nearly forty years later before any other educator suggested courses in journalism. When General Lee said that newspapers were educators and that they should be good educators, he was looking forward into the future.

Only a few days after the surrender of the South at Appomattox, when everybody on both sides was still excited and tense and angry and resentful, General Lee gave some advice to a young Confederate officer, who had been a member of the bold, reckless Moseby Rangers. For a short time after Lee's surrender, there had been wild talk that the war could be kept up by Confederate soldiers taking to the mountains and waging guerrilla warfare from there, as the Moseby Rangers had done. But when this young officer came to ask General Lee's advice, the General was wholeheartedly against the idea. He said it would make daily life no more than a nightmare of fighting.

Then the desperate young officer asked him, "What *shall* we do?"

Lee answered steadily, "Go home. All you boys go home and begin to build up what has been broken by the war."

Once in those last years of his life, someone asked him why he came to spend his days and nights working hard at a desk in an obscure, poor, educator's office. He said, "I have led American young men in war, and have seen them lie dead on the battlefield. I now think it my duty to help them to learn how to do their best in life."

ULYSSES S. GRANT

"Yes, they'll need their horses to get in their spring crops."

Years ago, in our high school, one of the younger boys came down with a dreadful attack of polio. He was very sick and for a long time badly crippled by paralysis. He never recovered completely. He walked and he ran, but some of his muscles never were wholly normal. He could not move fast, with the easy, flexible vigor of the rest of his companions. Yet he became one of the most reliable basketball players our school ever had, and helped our team win many a hard-fought game. In brains and courage and determination and quickness of "basketball thinking," he had qualities which made him a first-rater in spite of some stiffened muscles in his legs. We are proud of his example, we are still being helped by it. Every time a student in our school meets a setback—as everybody does once in a while—the memory of that boy helps him keep his chin up.

The story of our basketball player makes me think of the career of Ulysses S. Grant. I do not mean the whole of that career. In his later years, as President, he was not at all wise or successful.

That was sad. It is always a pity when someone fails at a job for which he is not fitted. But the mistakes of those clouded eight years should not blind us to his magnificent record when he was called to undertake a task which he fully understood and which no one else could have carried through as well as he did. So I think a fair verdict on his life is: "He was a poor President. But just the same he was a great man." He had proved it. The general who led the Union Army to victory in the Civil War earned our gratitude as one of our country's most famous military heroes. Even more, he earned that gratitude at the war's end by his great-hearted humanity toward the brave and gallant losers—the Army of Northern Virginia.

Like our country high-school boy, young Ulysses started out with a good many handicaps. He was not handsome or impressive-looking. In fact, to most people the stocky, plain, rather small man seemed very ordinary. He was not especially bright in his studies. When Ulysses was born, his father (of a New England family) was a farmer in Ohio in 1822, and not a prosperous farmer either. Ulysses was appointed to the West Point Military Academy in 1839 and stood only twenty-first in a class of thirty-nine students. When he graduated, the Mexican War was going on, and he served in it as an officer. But by 1854 he didn't seem to be getting any-where in the Army, so he resigned and went into farming and real-estate work in Missouri. But he didn't make much of a go at that. By 1860 he had given it up and was working as a clerk in his father's small leather store. By anything he had done to the age of thirty-eight, nobody could have guessed what he really was, in personality. People who knew him then respected him because he was honest and hard-working; but not many people knew him.

And then the horrible disaster of the Civil War broke out. Any man with military training was needed by his country. The clerk in the leather store was a West Point graduate, so he was called back to serve in the Army. What kind of officer did he turn out to be?

Well, as far as looks go, he stayed just the same—ordinary. Some of the other Army officers wore extra-fine uniforms, so that

anybody with one look at them would know their rank. Grant wore a plain uniform right through the war. He never thought about his looks. He thought about what had to be done.

Another officer wrote home a memory of General Grant. One night, during a rapid, forced march, his unit was crossing a stream on a pontoon bridge. Grant sat there on his horse, in his blue uniform, watching the men pressing across the swaying boat bridge. It was black night, but by the flare of torches the marching soldiers saw him to be their commanding officer. Many officers of high rank liked to be cheered by the soldiers. And of course the soldiers knew this. But nobody dreamed of wasting any breath that night on cheering General Grant. He kept his mind focussed on what was needed at that hour. Not on himself. He might have been a traffic cop for all he said, for all he looked. He kept calling out, "Close up the ranks, men. Hurry over." His job was to get them over the river as rapidly as possible, and he kept his mind on the job. That turned out to be one of his great gifts—a ball player would say he had a tremendous ability to keep his eye on the ball.

But this driving, steel-like determination of Grant's to get things done didn't mean blindness to the awfulness of what was being done. After the ghastly horror of the Battle of Shiloh, he could have lain down for the night in a warm, dry room under a roof. But the wounded men were being brought in under that roof for surgical care, and Grant suffered so terribly at the sight and sound of their pain that he went out and slept all night under the icy rain.

Yet he was the general who saw with his brain that to finish the war was the best way to end the misery, and it was his determination which pushed it through. By 1865, the Federal government had such faith in the abilities of the simple, homespun general that Grant had more than one million soldiers under his command. And General Lee and his army surrendered to him at Appomattox.

Then, from this everyday American came out a beautiful gesture of forward-looking human sympathy which none of us must ever forget. At the end of the Civil War it might have been possible legally, following a clause in the American Constitution, to treat the defeated Southerners as traitors. But President Lincoln and the Federal government had given General Grant the power to make humane terms when General Lee surrendered. The men of the Southern army were not to be hanged, not imprisoned; they were to be allowed to go back to their homes and live there quietly so long as they did nothing against the Federal government.

When General Grant wrote out these terms, they obviously gave General Lee a great relief. "This will have a very happy effect on my army," he said earnestly. He signed the statement of complete surrender to the North. General Grant wrote his big, powerful "U.S. Grant" at the bottom of the few simple clauses. That was all. The agonizing ordeal was over. The War between the States had come to an end.

So far, the small, ordinary-looking man in the dusty blue Union uniform had acted only on the authority which the Federal government had given him. But a new question came up. On this he made his own decision, in his own words. They were never written out and signed, but they have never been forgotten. Every one of us remembers them.

General Lee told him—something he had not known—that the horses used by the Southern army belonged to the soldiers themselves. Would it be possible, he asked, to allow those soldiers not to surrender their horses along with all the other Confederate arms to the victorious Army of the North, but to ride them back to their home farms?

General Grant had been a farmer on a small home farm and knew from experience how life looks to such hard-working men. What he did during the night after Shiloh tells us that there was something deep and compassionate under his commonplace outer appearance. In a great inner surge, his heart fused with his steel-like ability to keep his brains focussed on his real purpose. In that moment, the able professional soldier became a statesman. He saw, as a statesman must see, as few military men ever see, that victory is not an end but a means to a purpose far greater than victory. With the ink not yet dry on his signature as a victorious general, he lifted up his eyes to look beyond success into the welfare of the whole nation.

His first gesture was to help unlock the iron doors of hostility which might shut his country into the angry past.

In the plain, ordinary words he always used, he told General Lee he would give orders to the Federal officers in charge of the surrender to turn over a horse or a mule to any Confederate soldier who claimed to own one.

He looked across at Lee. "Yes, they'll need their horses to get in their spring crops," he said quietly, pushing open the door to the American future.

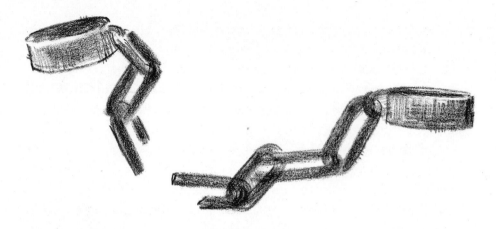

GEORGE WASHINGTON CARVER

The man who did most with the least.

The little Negro boy born just about a century ago came into this world with as little of his own as ever a baby had. He never saw his father, who had been a slave on a nearby plantation. And he never remembered seeing his mother. She belonged to the Carvers. She had been sold to them like a horse or a cow; but in the Missouri bushwacking during the last months of the Civil War she had been carried off by armed raiders stealing whatever they could lay their hands on, and nobody ever knew what had become of her. All that her baby boy had to remember her by was some infrequent chance reference . . . as once when Mrs. Carver was pleased with his neatness in sweeping the cabin floor and said, "Why I do believe you take after your mother. She did her work well."

By rights he didn't have a name of his own. There is no official record of birth or christening. Nobody bothered about such details for a Negro slave baby. As he grew older he learned to answer to the name George. The Carvers must have picked it out for him.

But dark as most of his prospects seemed, they were brightened by two pieces of good fortune. One of these was the fact that the Carvers, his mother's owners, were not native-born Americans. As children their minds had not become set by the talk of playmates and elders until they accepted without question the widespread assumption that all Negroes are inferior to all whites. They were Germans, the Carvers were, and they had come to America along with a great many other liberal-minded fellow citizens because they felt the Old Country was ruled by tyrannical despots, while the United States, they had heard, offered freedom and justice to everyone. Some of their ideas about freedom and justice did not fit at all well with the customs of the backward Missouri community where they settled. "They talk as crazy as if they were Abolitionists . . . almost." So rang their neighbors' gossip about them. However, the Carvers were hard-working people. They managed to get along not too well and not too badly on their little farm in the woods. And at least in their own home they were able to carry out their generous impulses. They felt that the little Negro boy and his brother Jim, who had fallen into their care by chance, were children—real human children—and they gave them as good protection as they would have given any children. When the boys grew older they ate at the same table as the Carvers and listened to their conversation.

Even more important than his sheltering foster parents was the second piece of good fortune. It was the surest bringer of happiness any human being can have, a wonderful something in his brain, born with him, guiding and driving him all his life—the craving to learn, to find out, to understand.

At first he had no books at all. That didn't matter. He looked sharply at everything around him with his bright dark eyes. He watched people do things he wanted to do—there was just about nothing which he didn't want to try—and his brain had the great gift of making his hands copy in the right order the motions his eyes observed. Once, so the story is told, when Mrs. Carver was knitting a scarf, he sat down on the floor near her feet and stared a long time at the way she twisted the wool on and off her knitting needles. He kept up this watching for several days until he thought he had mastered the trick of it. Then he went out and rummaged in the woodshed, found the wing feathers of an old hen eaten some weeks before because she had stopped laying, stripped two of the strongest quills, and there he had a pair of knitting needles. Raveling out some wool from a scrap of old stocking he found lying around, he went back and began to knit for himself. In time he learned to knit very well, and also to crochet.

One after another, George learned all the housekeeping jobs. One of them he did especially well. Like most women, Mrs. Carver usually kept plants growing in pots on her window sills. She soon noticed that when she let George take care of them they flourished and blossomed much better than they had ever done for her alone. She passed the word on to her friends, and whenever their plants began to look sick they asked help from George, because he seemed able to bring them back to life and health. Even when he was just a little boy they used to call him "the plant doctor." They said he had a "knack" for making things grow. Of course it was a great deal more than a knack. He had concentrated all his attention on noticing just what sort of soil, how much water, and how much sunshine gave the best results for each sort of plant. So, naturally, when he saw one of them stunted, with leaves beginning to turn yellow, he had pretty good ideas about what was needed to bring it back to health. But people were correct in calling him a "plant doctor." Only he wouldn't be ready to begin his lifework in any serious way until he had a great deal more experience and education. Experience was easy. Anyone with George Carver's observing eyes and organizing brain would learn plenty from any sort of life, anywhere. But formal education was a problem.

After slavery was abolished, in most communities some sort of elementary schools were set up for Negro children. When he was ten years old, George had the chance to go to one of them. A very rough-and-ready kind of school it was, a log cabin jammed much too full with dark-skinned pupils, with too few books and a teacher who wasn't very interested in his job. As usual, George made the best out of the little offered him. Very quickly he learned how to use the wonderful keys of reading and writing to unlock the treasures stored up in books. When he couldn't find books to practice on he went ahead by himself with any scrap of printed paper he could pick up. The pictures on advertisements were a great help in learning words and their meaning.

By and by this first crowded little school could teach him nothing he didn't know already. The Carvers let him go to the nearest settlement where there was a real school . . . no great improvement on the first one, but with better teaching and more books. He had no money, so he earned his board and lodging by working for a Negro woman who lived close to the school. She was a laundress, and it wasn't long before George was a master hand at washing clothes absolutely clean and starching them, as the fashion was in those days, so that a woman's skirt would stand up by itself with all the petticoat ruffles perfectly smooth, while gentlemen's shirts were stiff and shiny . . . you could almost see your face reflected by their high-polish gloss finish. Another of his part-time jobs to pay for board and lodging was as cook's helper, and again he didn't stay long washing raw vegetables and scouring pots and pans. In no time he was as good as his boss at broiling and roasting, making sauces and soups, everything flavored just right, tasting extra good.

So it was that during his teen-age wandering about the states near Missouri, from one place to another where there seemed a chance to get ahead with his schooling, he had two ways of earning his living. He never had any difficulty getting and keeping a job as household helper or cook in someone's kitchen. Food and lodging and some of his clothes were always provided for this sort of work; and that went a long way to make up for low wages in dollars and cents. Or, when he needed free time of his own to attend high-school classes, he always managed to find some little cabin he could rent for almost nothing because it was such a poor place that nobody else wanted it. After he had cleaned it up— he always kept everything around himself spotless—he paid his expenses and put by a bit more as savings for the future by doing fine laundry work for the families who belonged to that town's "high society."

Since he was a good cook he always had enough wholesome food to eat, because raw material for what goes into any meal— meat, eggs, potatoes, bread, milk—can be bought for only a fraction of what a restaurant has to charge for the finished product. George did the work for himself. He used dead branches picked up for nothing as the fuel for his kitchen fire. So he kept healthy and busy. His only question was "What next?" He never doubted that "more and more education, more and more study" was the right answer. But how was that to be managed?

When he was a little over twenty years old, he felt himself ready to step forward toward the future. There was a college in the Minnesota town where his roving life had taken him. He was sure that by washing and ironing clothes he could earn his own living cost and have enough money left over to pay the low tuition rates usual in the eighteen eighties. He was also sure that in school, one way and another, he had learned enough to pass entrance examinations. So, full of joyful excitement at the prospect of learning subjects far in advance of any he had yet studied, he went to the office marked "Entrance Applications" and said he would like to join the freshman class. The college official looked at him over his spectacles and answered casually, "But we don't take niggers here."

It makes me feel both sad and sick to write out the description of that brief interview. I can't just brush it off as a case of injustice by one solitary coarse-grained bureaucrat. I know well enough that Carver wouldn't have had better success at almost any other American college. Very likely the refusal might have been phrased more gently. The result would have been the same. In those days most doctors and educators were convinced that Negro children could learn pretty well up to a certain age—some put it at their thirteenth, others at their fifteenth year—but later than that something about their brains or the shape of their skulls made it impossible for any of them to go further. *Impossible!* It was a kindness to them not to let them break their hearts by trying. So far as I can find out there wasn't a shadow of adequate scientific evidence to support this theory. Somebody had said it was so. Others repeated what they had heard. Finally only a few—a very few—"cranks" doubted its truth.

It is queer how such fixed ideas get around and are believed by a great many people who won't take the trouble to check them against facts. Back in the early nineteenth century plenty of eminent teachers and college professors issued solemn warnings against women students taking up the study of mathematics. "Much too difficult," they insisted. "The weak feminine intellect cannot grasp algebra and geometry. The attempt will certainly bring on *brain fever.*" It's lucky that idea had been given up before Madame Curie came along. Otherwise the world might have had to wait a while for the development of radioactivity.

Race and national prejudice has had an uglier history. There have always been a certain number of mean-spirited Americans who have tried to puff their importance by shouting that our fine old traditions are being degraded by waves of immigrants—"the scum of the earth" . . . "dirty bogtrotters" . . . "Dagos" . . . "Chinks" . . . "Hunkies" . . . "Wops" . . . "Kikes!" That sort of talk still flares up occasionally, but mostly it had died down as each group of new citizens had proved that it follows pretty closely the world-wide human mixture . . . some bad, the big majority just about average, a few very good indeed.

Of all the minority groups, intelligent Negroes have been most hampered. The doctrine that African blood causes inferior brains and character was too handy an excuse for slavery to be overlooked, and it was vehemently preached for more than two centuries following 1619. The credit for convincing every fair-minded observer that nothing in their physical makeup prevents the colored races from thinking and reasoning at a high level is shared by many Negro pioneers. Among them George Carver is outstanding. Keen minds and brave hearts were needed for that struggle. Carver had both.

What was Carver feeling as he walked out of that college office? We can guess that at first he felt stunned and strangled. He never mentioned this experience in any letter which has been preserved. For this part of the story the only information we have comes from a biography written many years later by a fellow professor who had heard a great deal about his early life. We do know what he did. He tried again.

That happened later in the neighboring state of Iowa. Once again Carver screwed up his courage and asked to be admitted at Simpson College. This time the white man behind the registration desk asked him some questions about high-school subjects, thought a while, and then—it came like a thunderclap to the waiting ears—he said, "All right, my boy, we'll give you a chance."

A chance was all George Carver ever asked. He threw himself into his studies. Gracious, how he worked! His record was so

high that after graduation he had no difficulty in moving on for advanced study in agriculture at Iowa State College. Again his record was brilliant. Professor Wilson (later to be U.S. Secretary of Agriculture) said of him, "He is certainly one of the brightest, most intelligent, and most promising students I have ever had in my life."

Working in a good laboratory, guided by well-trained professors, he began to understand how the many separate facts about plant growth he had been observing for so many years could be grouped together to show the truth of a few general laws. Instead of a random jumble in his mind, they were forming a closely connected pattern. He labored to make that pattern larger, more complete, pushed forward by the true scientist's driving need to find answers to those continual questions. Why? Why? Why?

Iowa State was delighted to add him to its college faculty. He taught there for three years. Meanwhile his reputation grew. Several northern colleges of high standing offered him positions at good salaries, but he refused them all. Finally came the offer he had been waiting for. Tuskegee Institute, one of the first centers of what is called higher education opened to Negroes, had little money or equipment but a great need for able teachers. Would he consider taking the post of agriculture professor there?

"Yes," he replied to President Booker T. Washington. "It has always been the one great ideal of my life to be of the greatest good to the greatest number of 'my people' possible, and to that end I have been preparing myself for these many years: feeling as I do that this line of education is the key to unlock the golden door of freedom to our people."

In 1896 Tuskegee had been struggling along for fifteen years. It didn't look much like a college . . . just a few rough buildings, some of them with earthen floors, set on the corner of a run-down farm. Although this was Carver's first visit to Alabama he didn't need to stop and look around investigating conditions. He knew what was wrong from reading U.S. Agriculture Department reports. All over the "Deep South" the soil had been worn out by continued planting of a single cash crop, cotton; and what few fertile pockets might be left here and there were certainly not rented to Negro share-croppers. The new professor of agriculture got right down to fundamentals. No land anywhere could be more sterile than the fields around the Institute. Bringing them back into production would be the surest way to drive home the theory of his classroom lectures.

Theory, of course, was not left out. Every step in the campaign was explained in words simple enough for the band of eager student-laborers to understand, something like this:

Crops can't make a living on just clay or sand. They shrivel up and die unless their roots can reach some decayed vegetable matter . . . what the books call "humus." It's the same old endless chain: today's life gets its start from what's left of yesterday's life. Some mighty useful crops can do well on lean soil. Sweet potatoes, with their starch and sugar, make wholesome food. A handful of peanuts give us a lot of nourishment, let alone making the farm land better instead of worse. We'll try raising these two. But though they don't need much humus, they've got to have a little. How can we set about finding some for them? Did you ever think that one trouble with this hot, moist climate is that what you don't eat at once spoils the day after? Well, the one way to get along—always—is to figure out a plan so you can make your drawbacks pay dividends. Our neighbors hereabouts aren't what I'd call neat housekeepers. Everywhere there are big piles of rotting garbage. You can have them for nothing and be thanked for hauling them away. Never mind how they stink. Spread them on our experimental plot. Plow them under and then plant peanuts and sweet potatoes. You'll see. After a year or two the dividends will come along.

They did come along. The carefully kept accounts of the station farm, starting with a loss of $2.50 per acre, in seven years showed a net yearly profit per acre of $75.

When he came, Tuskegee Institute had no laboratory at all. Carver went right ahead with his experiments using homemade equipment—bottles and cracked chinaware picked up on the rubbish heaps—growing many different kinds of plants in old tin

cans, observing and noting down the effect of adding a pinch of this or that fertilizer to the rich compost earth he had made out of rotten watermelon rinds and other garbage. The knack which had earned him the boyhood nickname of "plant doctor" was still with him, but now his progress was no longer an affair of trial and error. His native hunch was guided by those years studying agricultural chemistry at Iowa State. Soon his ideas were far in advance of anything learned from books or lectures.

No matter how occupied he was with research problems, he always found time for direct personal teaching. The young women at Tuskegee were very bad cooks. He went right into the kitchen and worked with them. Can you imagine a professor of botany showing the home economics class how to fricassee chicken and bake corn bread! And he used their aroused attention to preach sound principles of nutrition. They must break away from the harmful, long-established custom of letting their menfolks eat nothing but "hog and hominy." He gave each of them a plot in the Institute farm to practice raising green vegetables. "When you have a home of your own," he told them, "set your garden patch close to the cabin door, where it will be handy to reach. And always water it with your dirty dish water; there's a lot of plant food in dishwater." In less than two generations, this campaign for a balanced diet, so authorities tell us, had brought about a marvelous improvement in health and vigor among Southern farm families.

Before long he had a better laboratory, though not an expensive one. He never needed that. Working in it, he took especial pleasure in finding some practical way to improve living standards among poor colored people . . . how, for instance, their dingy little cabins could be made cheerful by the many bright colors of an indoor paint made out of rotten sweet potatoes!

But the real test—the work which made him internationally famous—lay ahead. The boll weevil, continually widening its circle of destruction, was putting an end to cotton growing in many sections of the Old South. Fearing bankruptcy from the new menace, farmers, both white and Negro, were turning to new crops and finding—just as Carver had shown with his Tuskegee experiments—that their harvests increased abundantly, year by year. The very success of this program brought on a new crisis. More and more peanuts and sweet potatoes were being raised than could possibly be used for human food. What else could be done with them? Carver set himself to find out. The results were astonishing, stupendous! In case after case his creative imagination was able to sketch out a method by which large-scale industry could make a profit by transforming an unwanted surplus of raw material into a salable product.

A detailed account of everything he accomplished during his forty-seven years at Tuskegee would fill a thick volume. There is space here only to list in bare outline a few of his most striking achievements

By increasing the yield of sweet potatoes from 40 to 226 bushels per acre and thinking up 118 ways to use the enormous resulting total, he established an important money-earning southern crop. In 1945 the manufacture of vinegar, stock food, molasses, synthetic rubber, among a great many other useful products, furnished a ready market for the *68 million* bushels raised.

Where cotton could still be grown to advantage—in Africa, Australia, and parts of our own country—the "Carver Hybrid Seed" increased the yield from ⅓ bale to as much as 1¼ bales per acre . . . with an extra profit from oil, now pressed from the seed and forming under various trade names the mainstay of every American kitchen.

By careful drying (dehydration) he showed how to preserve the life-giving vitamins of many perishable vegetables.

He pioneered the introduction of soy beans on our midwest farms. Today that crop runs to 370 million bushels.

The 300 new commercial uses his research opened for the 1½ billion pounds of peanuts now raised range all the way from cheese and coffee substitutes, flour, dyes, ink, wood stains, insulating board, and poultry raising on litter from the shredded hulls to soothing oil for massage in polio treatment, and baby food which has saved countless lives in the Congo and other hot districts lacking refrigeration, where goat's and cow's milk sours almost at once.

What did the world think of him? What did people say about him? The verdict of praise was unanimous. Here are a few examples.

The United States Department of Agriculture rated Carver as "an authority on soil and plant life . . . an unfailing and strictly accurate source of information." He was elected "Honorary Fellow" of the British Society of Arts, received the Spingarn Medal (Kansas) for distinguished research in agricultural chemistry, also the Theodore Roosevelt Medal for distinguished service in the field of science, the first annual award of the Catholic Congress of the Southern States, the Edison Award for the Advancement of Science and Education. The *Progressive Farmer* magazine chose him as the "Man of the Year." The University of Rochester gave him the degree of Doctor of Science. He was elected to membership in the Honorary Society of Kappa Delta Pi.

He was promised a very high salary if he would transfer his work to the Thomas A. Edison Laboratories. Achiemento University in the Gold Coast Colony (now Ghana) offered him the post of department head, its president saying: "A man like him with ample facilities could work wonders in Africa." Carver thanked them both, but preferred to carry on what he had begun at Tuskegee. Henry Ford named his school for colored children after Carver, and invited him to dedicate the Ford Dietetic Laboratory at Dearborn, Michigan. The state of Missouri set up a marker at his birthplace.

A writer in a leading British magazine sums up his long career perfectly in a few words. "It is a great loss to us that we have no one like him in England. If I were asked what living man had the worst start and the best finish, I would say . . . Doctor Carver."

Carver, of course, was a genius, and genius is a mysterious quality. We can and do admire him, but we cannot really understand. Still less can we hope to lift any part of our plain ordinary lives up to the high level of his success story.

Nevertheless there is always a lesson for us packed away somewhere in any true account of human achievement, and we can find one here. How about that second college director of admissions? Since his name has been forgotten, let's turn to him for inspiration in moments of doubt. He didn't know that the young Negro across the desk from him was going to turn out a genius. He must have been tempted to guard against possible friction or criticism by saying that "unfortunately no vacancies are left in the next freshman class," or some other polite form of brush-off.

Suppose he had answered "No." Perhaps Carver would have fought his way to the front somewhere else . . . perhaps. But isn't it just as likely that this second refusal could have been the last straw . . . that the world would have kept a competent cook and laundryman, and lost a creative agricultural scientist?

Well, he didn't say "No," for he had that priceless sort of mind that doesn't slam the door on the face of a new idea, but honestly tries to give it the chance and the time it needs to prove whether or not it has value. So I do hope he was still alive, able to sit in the front row at the 1928 celebration in that small Iowa city. I wouldn't blame him for being a little proud of himself, for feeling that he deserved a share in the applause when it was announced from the platform that while nothing of importance could be added to the long list of honors already earned by the celebrated Guest of the Day, Simpson College wished to express the honor it had gained for *itself* by being the first to admit him as a student, and therefore was proud to bestow the honorary degree of Doctor of Science on its most distinguished son . . . George Washington Carver.

JOHN WOODWARD PHILLIP

"Don't cheer, boys. The poor devils are dying!"

I must have dozed off in my chair that afternoon, for what I saw was too strange to be anything but a dream. It seemed as if I had been lifted high into the air and was looking down at all the people in the world. There they were, millions of them, shoving and pushing each other about, a big formless mob, swaying from side to side, or walking in aimless circles. I could see that they were lost in a jungle so thick that no matter how hard they tried, they couldn't force their way through it. "Why don't they make up their minds about where they want to go?" I thought. "If they all work together they might trample down a path out into open country—but I suppose that is too much to expect from their excited and confused human brains."

Then some clouds shut me off from the earth, and when they cleared, the scene below was changed. The jungle was still there, fencing in a baffled crowd of men, women, and children. But these were not the same as those I had seen before. They were dressed in skins, and some of them carried stone war clubs. Time must have jumped backward, so that now I was looking at the world as it was many thousands of years ago. Next, with the spinning of the earth far below me, the centuries began to move quickly ahead, and after a while it was plain to me that the human multitudes were not staying in the same spot—not quite. A long trail lay behind them where they had blindly pushed and shoved and stumbled along. In spite of their confusion, they were doing just what I thought impossible for them. They were making a path slowly— oh so slowly!—toward where they really wanted to go. Where was that? They were trying to move away from barbarism—trying to reach civilization.

Don't ask me how I knew all this—anything can happen in a dream. And possibly this one did not spring from pure fancy. I had been reading many books written by learned experts on subjects with long names—such as anthropology, ethnology, archeology—all dealing with the development of our race. So it is quite likely that my dream resulted from my storyteller's mind unconsciously trying to put the dry facts of their research into a living picture.

By that time I was half awake and the rest of my thoughts were a jumble. What had seemed so vivid to me during my sleep was all mixed together with what I had read and thought so much about. I kept repeating it to myself, so that it would not fade out of my mind as dreams often do. "It's like this," I was saying. "It always happens the same way. Before the crowd can move ahead at all, one of the marchers must get a message from somewhere. No one knows where it comes from, but he hears it ringing in his ears. He feels an impulse to leap up high enough so that he can look over the underbrush and catch sight of far-off sunlit mountains. Then his whole body begins to glow with light. He shouts, stretches out his arms and points. It lasts only a minute or so. His light goes out. He drops back to the ground and begins pushing and shoving as before.

"But the minute counts! Sometimes what he shouts is heard by the others, and though they can't really understand, they remember that one flash of light over their heads—and the pointing arm. They move a few steps forward. Sometimes also they keep the memory of that flash of light long enough to tell their children and grandchildren about it."

I was wide awake now. I reached for a pencil and started to tell my grandchildren—for that is how I think of all young readers —about one such man and what he shouted in his single moment of clear vision. He was an officer in the American Navy. He never did much beyond the ordinary routine of his duty. But something he did do. Once he gave forth light—not much—but some. And real light.

John Woodward Phillip was twenty-one years old and had just finished his training at Annapolis when the Civil War broke out. During the next four years he served with the blockading fleet, cruising along the coast from Virginia to Florida, trying to close Southern ports and prevent European supplies from getting through to the Confederate Army. In this necessary but not at all exciting task he carried out all orders given to him promptly and efficiently, and finished the war with a good record.

Next came fifteen years of stagnation while our country let its Navy run down. However, Phillip stayed on, and some position was always found for him on one or another of the ships still in commission.

About 1880 Congress woke up to the fact that the old wooden-hulled vessels had just about rotted away. Money was appropriated and work started on a modern Navy—"ironclads" they were called, though there wasn't much iron used in them. Their big guns, turrets, and armor plate were all made of specially hardened steel. This was a tremendous undertaking calling for almost as great a change in the old fixed ideas about naval design as the building of atomic-powered submarines today.

It shows how highly John Phillip was regarded that he was put in charge of the Boston Navy Yard with a large number of men under him doing highly skilled work in construction. As always, he was entirely adequate to the responsibility. The mechanical work turned out at the Navy Yard was well done. The morale among the workers was excellent.

1898 brought the Spanish-American War—the first real test of our sea power in eighty-odd years. How would our ships stand up? Nobody knew. And what about the Spanish fleet? Nobody knew either. It also had not been tested for years, but the rumor was that it might be formidable. There was a good deal of nervous alarm in our seaboard cities when the news got around that Admiral Cervera had slipped past our scout ships, had crossed the ocean, and was now anchored in the harbor of Santiago, Cuba, at that time a Spanish possession. But before he could refuel and start to raid our coast or sink our Army transports, whatever his plans may have been, he was bottled up there by six of our best armed vessels, standing guard, waiting for him to come out through the narrow channel and fight. One of these, the battleship *Texas*, had John Phillip in command. What a relief that must have been for him after his long patient waiting. It had been over thirty years since he had heard a shot fired in anger. Soon he was to hear plenty.

For our land troops were closing in on Santiago. The city must fall before long. Cervera, the Spanish admiral, had the choice of waiting to be captured at anchor or of making a run for it. On the morning of July 3 he came out.

The men on Phillip's ship, nerved for the battle, rushed to their stations, ready to the last detail. With his professional fighting-man's foresight, he had trained them until they acted like the parts of a smoothly running machine. A Spanish cruiser appeared, drew near threateningly. Phillip's sonorous voice gave the command to fire. A deafening burst roared from the big cannon, a constant *bang, bang, bang* from the secondary batteries. A blinding cloud

of black smoke settled down over everything, for smokeless powder had not yet been invented. A few scattered feeble shots from the Spanish ship came through the smoke, doing no harm to the American man-of-war. What was happening? Tense and quivering, the crew of the *Texas* kept on firing. Nothing was to be seen. Then a breeze springing up blew a rift in the night-black smoke. Through it they all caught a glimpse of the Spanish enemy careening wildly to one side—badly struck, and headed for the beach. Her flag had been hauled down. Phillip ordered the "cease fire," and brought the *Texas* up close. Yes, the *Oquendo* (that was the name of the Spanish ship) was entirely disabled. Victory—an unheard-of completeness of victory! For an instant his crew, coming out from their battle stations, could not take it in, and stood stunned. Then a wild yell of exultation burst from them.

It was loud, but Captain Phillip's voice was louder. He had every right to rejoice in the victory. At one blow he had reached the great triumph which he had been trained all his life to live for. Up to that moment he had thought of war as a matter of drill, range-finding, navigation, and a thousand other technical details to be prepared for and put in use when needed. But now he saw that victory had a further meaning. Before him on the crippled *Oquendo* the black bodies of men were sliding down her tilted sides, dropping into the sea. One corner of his heart had not been hardened by all those years of training for battle. From that human heart came a cry of understanding.

He shouted, *"Don't cheer, boys. The poor devils are dying!"*

No one can claim that Captain Phillip accomplished much in changing the course of history. Not yet! I warned you that advance is always painfully slow. But maybe he did a little. For I did not forget his words, and now you will remember them. And there's a chance that you or your grandchildren will do something to clear up the world situation which my generation has left in such a mess.

You—whoever you are who is reading this book—must keep in your mind that what war really means can be stated in these simple words: "I know that you want to kill me, but I intend to kill you first." Think that over and decide whether a world run on that principle is one that you want to bring up a family in. If your answer is "No," don't keep your opinion to yourself. Go out and tell others about it. Don't be discouraged when people answer that there always have been wars, and you can't change human nature. When they say "human nature" they are thinking about human customs, and those are changing all the time. Back in the thirteenth century—and that's less than a minute ago, compared with the time which has passed since men first began to chip out flint arrows and spearheads—if one nobleman charged another with some crime (it might be plotting to kill the king and seize the throne for himself), they didn't argue the case before a judge and jury. No, they put on their armor and hacked at each other with swords or battle axes until one or the other was killed or asked for mercy. Everyone was positive that the result *proved* that the loser must be a liar and guilty. Of course, we see now that such a fight proved nothing except that one man was stronger or more clever with his weapons than the other. We don't settle private quarrels that way any longer. But for nations, mass slaughter is still considered all right—even a little glorious as a last resort.

The work I am asking you to undertake will not be easy. It is always hard to change established public opinion. Your road will be steep and rough. There will even be times—don't I know it, I who have lived through two earth-shaking wars?—when you yourself cannot be sure about what is right, what wrong. I am proud that both my husband and my son chose to serve their country. And yet—and yet—was either world war inevitable? It is hopeless, of course, to try to stop a war once the shooting has begun. It is too late then. But, looking back, I blame myself and my generation for not making a greater effort to ease the bad feeling before it became acute. Could we not have done more to force the statesmen on both sides to insist less on power politics and national pride, so that they could have come together in an open, reasonable spirit, accepted give-and-take compromises, worked toward world cooperation? For the time to stop a war is years *before* the armies are ordered to march.

It won't be long before you will be voting, and can help to stop the next war. You will not be alone. Thousands of good citizens will come forward to join in a "prevent war" crusade.

Here is one last word from an old woman who cares passionately about your future happiness. "Don't hang back because you are afraid that to make the effort successful will call for a lot of hard work. So it will. But think of the cost if it fails. Whether it is your son or the son of some foreign mother and father—the dead can never be brought back to life."

About the Author and Artist

Dorothy Canfield Fisher (1879–1958)—one of the most respected writers of our time—was a native of Kansas who returned to her family's home state, Vermont, for which she had great pride and love. Yet Mrs. Fisher had a truly cosmopolitan background and spirit. As Robert Frost wrote: "There was nothing she was happier in than storytelling in prose and speech unless it was doing good to everybody and anybody. She came from all directions from as far West as Kansas and from as far East as France." She held degrees from eight American universities, but her reputation was international—not only for her outstanding adult and children's books, which amounted to more than forty in all and which have been translated into many languages, but also for her real understanding of people and of the universal values of life. These qualities prompted her to write the works for children, *A Fair World for All, Our Independence and the Constitution,* and another children's classic, *Understood Betsy.*

Mrs. Fisher was for twenty-five years a member of the editorial board of the Book-of-the-Month Club, and in her memory the Club has set up an annual *Dorothy Canfield Fisher Library Award.* She was also a former president of the American Association for Adult Education, and former vice president of the Child Welfare Information Service and of the American Parents Committee. In 1951, she received The Constance Lindsay Skinner Award from the Women's National Book Association.

Ezra Jack Keats has illustrated many books, including *The Chinese Knew, The Indians Knew,* and *The Pilgrims Knew,* which were written by Tillie S. Pine and Joseph Levine, and the Danny Dunn stories by Jay Williams and Raymond Abrashkin. He attended New York schools and the Art Students' League and later taught at the Famous Artists' School in Westport, Connecticut. He spent a year in Paris and his on-the-spot research for book illustrations has taken him to many different locations, including Cuba and Scotland. Mr. Keats now lives in New York City.